# A NATURAL HISTORY OF MAN

*A Biologist's view of: birth and death; nature and nurture;
man and society; health and disease; immigration and emigration;
history and heredity; war and peace*

## J. K. BRIERLEY

HEINEMANN

LONDON

CHESTER COLLEGE

ACC. No. 812726 | DEPT. X

CLASS No. 599.9 BRI

LIBRARY

WITHDRAWN

Heinemann Educational Books Ltd
London  Edinburgh  Melbourne  Toronto
Singapore  Johannesburg  Auckland
Ibadan  Hong Kong  Nairobi

SBN 435 60132 6

© J. K. Brierley 1970
First published 1970

Part title illustrations by Vernon Lord

Published by Heinemann Educational Books Ltd
48 Charles Street, London W1X 8AH
Printed in Great Britain by
Butler & Tanner Ltd, Frome and London

To Ann

R37/11

1-75

BRIERLEY, J.K.
NATURAL HISTORY OF MAN
812726 01 572

# CHESTER COLLEGE LIBRARY

Author ....... BRIERLEY ........................

Title ... A natural history of man ...........

Class No. .... 572 ........ Acc. No. .... 812726 ....

This book is to be returned on or before the last
date stamped below

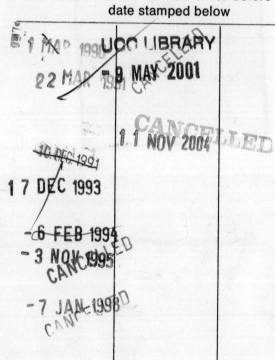

1 MAR 1990 UCC LIBRARY

22 MAR 1991 -9 MAY 2001

10 DEC 1991

1 1 NOV 2004 CANCELLED

17 DEC 1993

-6 FEB 1994

- 3 NOV 1995 CANCELLED

-7 JAN 1998 CANCELLED

# A Natural History of Man

By the same author

*Science in its Context*
*Biology and the Social Crisis*

# Author's Note
# and Acknowledgements

THIS book like its companion volume, *Biology & the Social Crisis*, is intended for the common reader and to provide a basis and background for discussion among sixth formers, both arts and science, and other young students. It is not an original book but is based on the work of many scholars. For those who wish to read more deeply a bibliography of books and papers consulted during the preparation of the book has been included.

No apologies will be made for the speculative reasoning found in certain parts of the book. One of the attractions of biology is that the subject can provide material which requires the expression of an opinion or point of view. I have tried to avoid oversimplification of the subject matter, to present differing viewpoints and to indicate the lines of demarcation between established teaching, developing knowledge and personal views, but compression has inevitably led to some oversimplification.

I should like to thank a number of people who have helped me in writing this book. First and foremost I owe a great debt to Professor C. D. Darlington F.R.S. for his interest. He has read the manuscript and generously lent me the proofs of his great book, *The Evolution of Man and Society*, to consult while writing Part 3. Here I describe a number of Darlington's new theories. For example that of 'directed' evolution of the brain and its selective cause (p. 38), and the theory of the origins of cultivators (p. 53). These interpretations of Darlington's may well be disputed in many details, and even in principle. Nevertheless I find them convincing and stimulating. I am grateful, too, to Sir Julian Huxley, F.R.S. for his encouragement and help. I should like to thank my former colleague at Manchester Grammar School, Mr F. C. Minns for a thorough and critical reading of the manuscript. My thanks are due, too, to Emeritus Professor J. D. Chambers, formerly Professor of Economic History at Nottingham University for his interest and for reading some of Parts 4 & 5, to Dr B. Fox, Consultant at the Charing Cross Hospital Medical School for checking the medical accuracy of the book, to Dr M. Sprackling for further help on the medical side of the book and to my wife who read the manuscript for clarity and sense and left it much improved. I am grateful to the numerous authors of the charts and tables acknowledged in the text.

None of the above however can be responsible for errors of fact or judgement which may be found in the book.

Nottingham. December 1969      JOHN BRIERLEY

# Contents

# Prologue

LIKE all present-day books on biology this one owes a debt to Charles Darwin. It was he who showed that man is an animal who can and must, if he wishes to understand himself, be investigated as other animals, by applying the whole battery of scientific methods to himself. This means that in his heredity and variation, in his physical, emotional and mental properties, his individual, social and racial characters, in his diseases, in his language, his religions and in his behaviour, he is a proper object of experimental study. And in some of these respects his evolution is subject to the same principles of natural selection as other animals.

It is, of course, easier said than done. No-one turns a hair at being asked in a census, his age, the size of his family and so on. And none of us minds much if comparisons are made about the working of our bodies with that of a dog or monkey. In the one case such investigations have taught us about population structure and in the other they have led to an understanding of the functions, for example, of our kidneys, our heart, our hormone-producing glands. And with this understanding has come control: medicine. But to suggest that altruistic behaviour, or that the parcelling out of living space, whether as between individuals, nations or 'blocks', have their roots firmly in the soil of our animal heritage, and that both have been developed by natural selection, is another matter. It goes against the grain to have our behaviour compared with that of baboons or rats. Just as the wife of the Bishop of Worcester felt over a century ago when the Bishop told her that Professor Huxley had announced that man was descended from the apes—'Descended from the apes! My dear, let us hope it is not true, but if it is, let us pray that it will not become generally known,' —we might want to dismiss the repellant thought that a quality like 'unselfishness' has evolved in us by the ruthless automatic mechanism of natural selection.

In any case why is all this knowledge about man important? Apart from its obvious medical and social significance, mainly because it is interesting. Knowledge of mankind too, if thought about, may lead to a greater understanding of ourselves and perhaps to greater tolerance and increased sensitivity to human diversity. Indeed if we press the case further it may help us to recognize and prevent the disrupted relationship between our own behaviour and the use of our environment though this is a pious hope.

Natural history is the scientific study of the ways of life of an organism and its life history. The natural history of man, then, is a vast subject which could embrace everything to do with man from his behaviour to his breeding systems, from his class structure to his dialects, from his ape-like origin to his many religions. This book however, concentrates on five main areas.

*Parts One* and *Two* provide the foundation for much of the rest of the book. Their object is to reveal what kind of animal man is.

*Part One* shows how vital statistics and other population data help, in a rough way, to map the patchy distribution of the human species, to chart man's density from place to place, to record something about his fertility, his changing marriage patterns and the diverse illnesses to which he succumbs. This we might describe as the mechanics of his natural history. But study of these data exposes a gross lack of knowledge about ourselves. In fact the base-line of information on such matters as population size, crude birth and death rates and what diseases men die of the world over is not a line at all but a series of dots and dashes.

*Part Two* comes down from the aerial view of man to flesh and blood, and beyond this to the genes. The concepts of 'nature and nurture' and homeostasis are examined. The latter embraces the mechanisms that automatically keep the body machinery working smoothly no matter whether it is baking hot or freezing cold. Our deep body temperature for instance varies less than 3°F no matter what the external temperature is like. This quality and others we shall describe, has allowed man to overrun the earth; its deserts, forests, high mountains and ice fields. It and others have made him into the great amateur of the animal kingdom, uncommitted to any specific niche in the environment. Man also has a diverse heredity. As an individual he fits more easily into environments that have been created by a similar heredity to his own. Both his homeostatic properties and his many and diverse gifts are determined by the genetic character of the fertilized egg.

The origins of man are considered in *Part Three* mainly to introduce some discussion of the past as an introduction to the present and the future. Early man is described and his great expansions over the world and how he adapted to climate, altitude and disease. The roots of the class system, the development and spread of agriculture, the creation of cities, population growth, destruction of habitat and migration of peoples and the origins of the breeding system are discussed. And many questions are posed. Why is the instinct against incest and other forms of close mating so strong? And, on the other side of the coin, why is wide cross-breeding between races and classes frowned upon? How did new peoples with the new capacities to domesticate the cereals and the wild animals originate and why did they originate in the evolutionary cradles of the Near East and Central America? What human and environmental qualities were necessary for the creation of cities?

At the roots of the invention of agriculture and indeed all human progress from the pebble tools of *Australopithecus* to the moon-junketing of the astronauts, we shall note a basic principle. It is the principle of a self-exaggerating effect with a positive feed-back which leads to continued change in one direction—the development of man's brain. Each invention, like tools, fire, and writing was the result of inherited abilities and each invention encouraged more ability of a similar kind. It sharpened the selection *against* those who could not exploit the new invention, widening the gap between gifted individuals, families, castes, tribes and nations and those not so gifted. We see the principle at work today in the advances of science. Every discovery exaggerates the differences between those countries who are and those who are not, capable of using it; the one forges ahead, the other lags. Inventions past and present have had an autocatalytic effect.

They have allowed the faster multiplication of those who could use them. And the inventions themselves favoured those who could teach others about them, and those who could learn. Better speech and nervous control became essential attributes for natural selection triggering other inventions and they in turn more brain-power. So the cycle went on, but always the development of the brain was driven in one direction; always 'man made himself'.

Next, in *Part Four*, the changing pattern of human disease is outlined with its different incidence among rich and poor, male and female, young and old and its relationship to the seasons. Old and new epidemics are described, from the death which came 'like black smoke' and which hurt 'like a burning cinder' (bubonic plague) to lung cancer and thrombosis. The barometers of socio-medical progress are examined: infant mortality, maternal mortality, expectation of life and the death rate. It is shown how these have changed over time and also how they differ now from country to country. The major patterns of death in the 'eight ages' of Western man are summarized. The last chapter in this part discusses the question, 'is health improving?' The conclusion reached is that in an ever-changing world, each period and each civilization will continue to have its burden of disease created by an unavoidable failure to adapt to the new environment.

*Part Five* looks at migration from the point of view of a biologist. It examines the *selective* action of migration with respect to the genetically determined properties of fertility and intelligence. Thus we shall see how the expulsion of thousands of Jews from Spain during the Inquisition impoverished that country genetically and may have contributed to its backwardness. Religious persecution there and elsewhere —in France with the Huguenots—set up a massive brain drain. In Britain today such a drain is diminishing the pool of talent, especially of scientists and engineers. If this rapid leak continues over many generations it could reduce our competence to the level of the Red Indians or the Eskimos; for with the brains go the breeding potential. We shall see too how, after the famine in the mid-nineteenth century, the fertility of Ireland was reduced by the exodus of the young and fertile. From nearly eight millions in 1846 its population approximately halved in the following 30 years and today still stands at less than half the peak number.

Mapping migration by blood genes helps to show, together with historical and other evidence, the origins and wanderings of people. Even sixty or seventy generations after their expulsion from Ancient

Palestine most of the Jews have retained their 'purity' by not inter-breeding too freely with other surrounding peoples. But the scattered Jewish populations the world over differ genetically from each other. Why should the Jews, who originated from one area, show such marked differences? The British, on the other hand, are a genetic soup, but with here and there a pile-up of blood genes which may represent traces of ancient populations. In particular the blood-gene O may trace the distribution of the red Celts of fiery-red hair, blue eyes and transparent, freckly skins; the AB and B blood types possibly pin-point in parts of Wales traces of the 'dark Iberian' populations—the black Celts—and perhaps reveal the remains of even older, Stone-Age populations. In Scotland these blood types could mark the remains of the tatooed fighting men, the Picts. Blood-gene A shows Viking traces in Eastern England and 'little England' in Pembrokeshire.

*Part Six* of the book briefly enters the highly controversial area of human aggression for two reasons: because war is a part of the natural history of man and is thus a fit study for examination by biologists, and for the more practical reason, that unless we do learn soon how to control human aggression we must live with the second to second risk of swift annihilation of our species by germ warfare or rockets. As will be shown the controversy centres on whether human aggression is inborn or culturally determined. From the evidence at our disposal we can draw only one certain conclusion. It is that, apart from trying to get population down to a reasonable density and stopping the irreversible extinction of plants and animals by chemical poisons and unthinking extermination, there is an urgent need for further research on the biology of animal and human behaviour particularly aggression. The fruits of this modest-sounding proposal may help to save us from mass suicide. But even when remedies have been discovered we shall still have to trust the politicians to use them.

# Part 1: The Mechanics of Natural History

# 1: Vital Statistics

' ALL that's living in this house now,' said Mrs Smith, 'is me, Dad,
Father, Charlie Boy, Dick, Eddie, Karen, Valerie and Colin.
Mum died last year of a stroke and left Father on his own, so
he came to us. I've lived here since 1945 when Dad and me married.
All the kids were born here, all eight of them. We've only six at home
though. Two are married with kids.'

What Mrs Smith said contains many of the essentials of 'vital
statistics'. That is, facts on such matters as live birth, death, foetal death,
marriage, divorce and adoption. Population censuses yield these data
by asking such bald questions as: 'what is the total number of completed years of the present marriage?'; 'what is the total number of
children still living?' and 'what is the total number who have died?'
The results of these data from all the countries of the world end up in
huge volumes such as *The United Nations Demographic Year Books*. To
the layman the information contained in such books appears dry as
dust but from them can be learned much about the conditions of life
of people in a certain country.

It is customary to gain information about the ways of the human
animal with the help of elaborate and continuing systems of record

keeping and 'representative statistics'. That is, a certain number of individuals are selected who are supposed to stand for the mass of people and attention is directed to them by asking them questions like the ones above. From this source can be learned their average length of life, their wanderings, their increase or decrease, the average age of marriage, the pattern of family building, what diseases people die of and at what ages, what diseases strike different trades and professions and much else.

Besides these vital events other 'demographic' data are obtained in population censuses which tell us about population size, its rate of growth from country to country, the size of cities and the size of rural populations, the racial composition, languages and religions of different countries and many more things about them. Vital statistics and demographic data, therefore, enable the biologist to build up a rough map of the life of a country and also fill in details about such matters as the birth–death cycle, just as he might build up a picture of the territories and habits of life of, say, a robin.


## AGE OF DEATH

To illustrate its use to the human biologist the results of some of this data is shown in the charts and graphs. Fig. 1 shows the changes over a century or more in the ages of death in Sweden, England and Wales, Mexico and among the Moslem population of Algeria. As judged by the populations of Algeria and Mexico, by 1940 only a tiny fraction of the world's population had achieved an expectation of life at birth achieved by the populations of England and Wales and Sweden. Most of the world was like that of Mexico or the Moslems of Algeria, living no longer than people in Western Europe lived in the Middle Ages. Within the last 20 years as the graphs show and Chapter 17 elaborates, the chance of a twentieth century death-rate has been given to the masses of the world. In 1940 the death-rate in Mexico was like that of England and Wales a century ago but in the ten years between 1940 and 1950 it decreased as much as did the death-rate in England and Wales during the half century between 1850 and 1900. Expectation of life is a useful indication of *socio-medical progress* and shows on a small scale what has happened in the past ten or twenty years to the life span of people in Latin America, Africa and Asia.

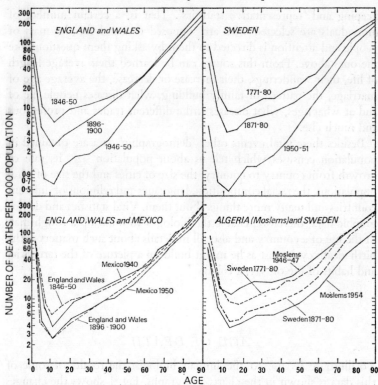

FIG. 1 Age-specific death rates per thousand per year for Sweden, England and
Wales, Mexico and the Moslem population of Algeria for various time periods
from 1771 to 1954. From an article by F. H. Dorn in *Human Ecology* (ed.
Bresler).

## BIRTH RATE

Fig. 2 shows that the birth-rate has altered little throughout most of
this area (compare with U.S.A.), standing at around 40 live births per
1,000 of population each year. The facts speak for themselves. Decreasing death-rates everywhere with birth-rates remaining high have led to
bursts in numbers, some of them striking. Even in countries like Puerto
Rico and Japan where birth-rate has sunk, the rate of natural increase
has altered little, owing to the sharp decline in mortality. Fig. 3 pre-
sents data collected by the United Nations in 1962 which show world
population changes 1920 to 2000. The big increases as expected will

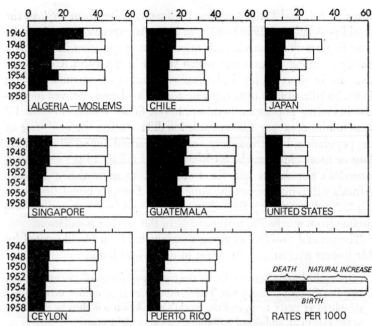

FIG. 2 Birth-rate, death-rate, and rate of natural increases per thousand for selected countries for the period 1946–58. From an article by H. F. Dorn in *Human Ecology* (ed. Bresler).

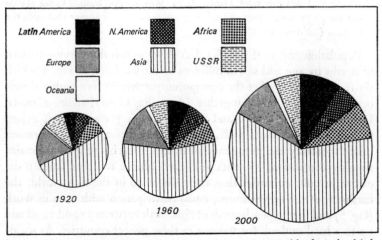

FIG. 3 World population changes, 1920 to 2000. From *Health of Mankind* (ed. G. Wolstenholme), Churchill, 1967.

come in Asia and Latin America, the former rising from 55% of the world population in 1960 to 62% in 2000. As a specific example, India is adding a million people each month to its population in spite of a family planning programme which started in the 1920s. Contraceptives are in short supply and a limited number are manufactured in India. Sterilization of men (by vasectomy) has largely proved ineffective in cutting population build-up. In one State, Maharashtra, the 1·2 vasectomies done per 1,000 population did not affect the birth-rate of the population, but if vasectomy could be carried out on all men with four or more children, the birth-rate would fall by 18 per cent. Latin America's population will rise from 6·5% to more than 9% while Africa's will remain about the same at 8%. Europe's population, with the U.S.S.R. will drop from 23% to 15% and North America's will decline from nearly 7% to about 5% of the world's population.

The general problem of rising numbers has been bleakly stated by Mr Robert McNamara, President of the World Bank:

> It required 1,600 years to double the world population of 250 million as it stood in the First Century A.D. Today, more than 3,000 million on earth will double in 35 years' time, and the world's population will then be increasing at the rate of an additional 1,000 million every eight years.
>
> A child born today, living on into his seventies, will know a world of 15,000 million. His grandson will share the planet with 60,000 million. In six and a half centuries from now—the same insignificant period of time separating us from the poet Dante—there will be one human being standing on every square foot of land on earth: a fantasy of horror that even the Inferno could not match.

Population and vital statistics data show us too the varying pattern of deaths by age and sex in different countries. Look at Fig. 4 which throws into sharp relief the contrasting patterns in five highly developed countries lumped together (Australia, Great Britain, Canada, Denmark, and U.S.A.) and five developing countries (Ceylon, Colombia, Egypt, Guatemala, Mexico). In the latter, after an enormous infant mortality the percentage of deaths in each age group remains roughly constant to 85 years and over. Notice too that women die earlier in poor countries than their sisters do in the rich world; the harshness of the environment, equal participation with men in work (Fig. 5) and the greater hazards of childbirth between 15 and 45 all add up to a hard outlook for women in these poorer countries. As sociomedical improvements come the charts will change shape and indeed must have changed since they were made in 1954.

DEATHS BY AGE AND SEX

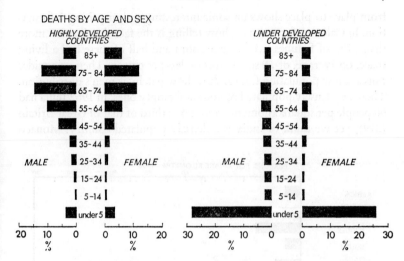

FIG. 4 Deaths by age and sex. From *World Health*, F. Brockington, Churchill, 1967.

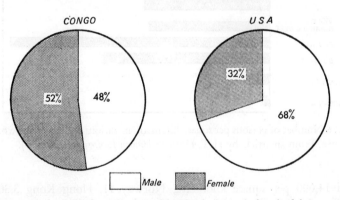

FIG. 5 Economically active populations: male and female labour. From *World Health*, F. Brockington, Churchill, 1967.

## DENSITY OF PEOPLE

A study of the greater density of people caused by the population increase is revealing. Fig. 6 shows how close the masses huddled in 1958 in various regions of the world. To map the density of the human animal

from place to place shows up some interesting and surprising information. In Calcutta for instance, how telling is the fact that in 1967 more
than 57% of families lived in one room and half of these had a living
space, on average, of 30 square feet or less per person. Then on a wider
canvas a few population figures show how patchy is man's distribution.
There are densely populated regions and empty ones. In 1962 India had
66 people per square kilometre, about one third of that of Great Britain
(219), yet we think of India as a densely populated country. Monaco

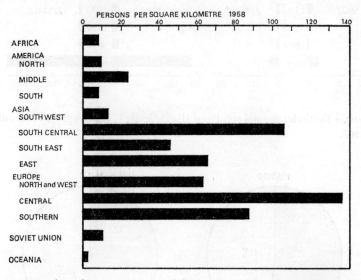

FIG. 6 Number of persons per square kilometre in various regions of the world
in 1958. From an article by H. F. Dorn in *Human Ecology* (ed. Bresler).

had 14,000 per square kilometre, Norway 11, Hong Kong 3,304,
Congo 2, Australia 1, Russia 10, Canada 2 and United States 20.
And statistics can tell us something about the economies of countries.
Egypt has an area of about 386,000 square miles and a population of
about 24 millions while Denmark has an area of about 16,000 square
miles and a population of $4\frac{1}{2}$ millions. The Danes have plenty to eat and
export large quantities of food yet the Fellaheen of Egypt go hungry.
Why? Because, as the maps will tell us, the arable land of the Nile
valley covers about the same acreage as Denmark, the rest, 370,000
square miles, is desert.

## FERTILITY POTENTIAL

Fig. 7 shows the different age groups found in Sweden (representing the affluent section of the world) and in the Moslem population of Algeria (representing the poorer world) in 1954. These data are some of the most important obtained in population censuses. What use are they to the biologist? Looking at the age structure of the Moslem population, about 40% of the people are *under* 15 years of age. The corresponding figure for Sweden is 24%. For Great Britain in 1956 it was

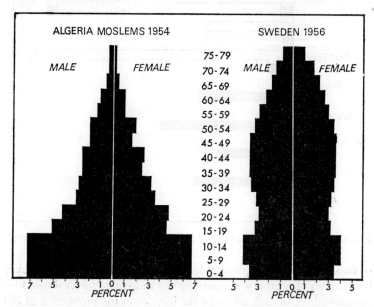

FIG. 7 Percentage distribution by age of the population of Sweden in 1956 and the Moslem population of Algeria in 1954.

22%, for the U.S.A. 27%. In 1968 *under 20s* formed 30·9% of the population in Great Britain; by 2000 they may represent a third.

People of this age (15–20) have a huge fertility potential for 25 to 30 years (spanning for women the reproductive period). Unless there is a sharp decline in birth-rate especially in Latin America and Asia, standards of living, education, indeed the whole quality of life will drop sharply. Anybody with teenage children knows to their cost, too, that these younger age groups demand more food than older age groups.

The charts in Fig. 7 also show how few people reach 40 and over in the 'poor' country compared with the rich. In Sweden and other technologically advanced countries people have learned to limit their numbers so that society here is made up of small units with an average

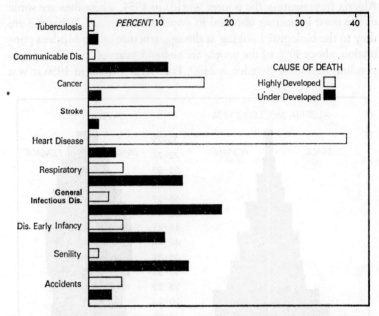

FIG. 8 Causes of death. From *World Health*, F. Brockington, Churchill, 1967.

of two children whose physical health is so good that infant mortality is a fraction of what it was a century ago and where survival past 40 is commonplace. In such countries the increase in the proportion of old people brings with it different biological and social problems. Fig. 8 makes a general point by showing the sharply contrasting causes of death in highly developed and under developed countries.

# 2: The Birth-Death Cycle

THE vital statistics which chart the fertility, marriage and death patterns of a population show us where we are and where we are heading. With this in mind, let us look at the British population, which is broadly representative of richer countries, in relation to three facets of the human life cycle: marriage, fertility and death.

Marriages are taking place at younger ages than before. In 1911 about 37% of men and 46% of women were married at 25 compared with 37% and 48% in 1931 and 60% and 80% in 1961. In addition, in 1961 men, whatever their age of marriage, were marrying girls about one and a half years younger than in 1931. In 1967 the average age of the groom was nearly 25 and the bride 22½. One might suppose that this choice of younger mates is a biological development linked with earlier maturity. But in fact the explanation is duller than this and seems to be a matter of supply and demand in the marriage market. Women are now in short supply compared with 1931 so men have to chase younger women to find enough partners.

Interest in fertility grew in the second half of the nineteenth century probably because the study of death (mortality) became a less pressing problem since people were living longer. Forecasts about birth-rate, as we know, are notoriously hazardous. Fig. 9 shows the pattern in the number of babies born over the last 20 years. Although not shown here, the level of births before the 1939–45 war was low, probably

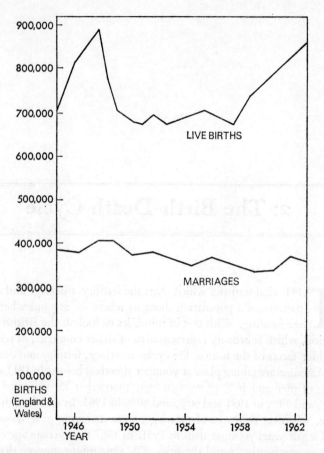

FIG. 9 The level of births. From 'Patterns and Trends in Recent British Population Developments' by P. R. Cox in *Biological Aspects of Social Problems* (ed. Meade and Parkes), Oliver and Boyd, 1965.

reflecting unemployment and worry about a bleak economic future; then came the post-war peak, then the fall, and then the new feature shown on the graph, of a steady and large rise in births since 1955, perhaps reflecting the leap out of wartime austerity. Note too that this substantial rise was not preceded by any corresponding increase in the number of marriages.[1] No-one but a prophet could have forecast this trend, but the implications for the British population are far-reaching. By 1963 the population had increased by two millions over expectation. In 1953 the forecast was made for 1963 of 45 million people in England and Wales. Actually it was 47 millions. For 2003, 46 millions were predicted but on *present* trends it will be 64 millions.

## FORECASTING FERTILITY

The nub of the problem of forecasting is how to predict 'total fertility'; that is the number of children born to an average woman by the end of her reproductive period. Clearly this is a tricky business, but before explaining it, a word about 'fertility'.

It has been reckoned that in the circumstances most favourable to reproduction (when every woman marries under 20, and surplus men are waiting to re-marry any widows), assuming the onset of infertility about 20 years after marriage, then 'total fertility' should be eight. This magic number is arrived at as follows. The probability of conception, allowing for some miscarriages and some temporary sterility during lactation, implies the birth of a child every $2\frac{1}{2}$ years of marriage: $20/2\frac{1}{2}$ equals eight! But 'total fertility' cannot be measured directly until the generation in question has reached the end of its reproductive period and this would be no use to the forecaster; the result is then a matter of historical interest. So to help him make his prediction he juggles with three factors which have been shown to be linked with fertility: the mother's age at marriage, length of time married and the date of the marriage.

Let us look at how completed family size has been associated with the mother's age of marriage and the date of her marriage. Women married under 20 during 1900–09 had an average of five children in all. Those married as young today have three. Those married at 25–29 in the early years of the century had nearly three children on average; now they have two. Fashions change. The effect of length–of–time–married on fertility shows that younger couples (under 20) necessarily take longer (over 20 years from the date of marriage) to complete their larger families compared with those who marry later (25–29). These older couples usually complete their families after around 16 years from

---

[1] A dramatic example of a leap in births was in New York State in 1967, nine months after widespread failure of electricity supply one night in 1966!

the date of marriage. Table 1 gives the raw data which warn that to try to predict the final size of a family from the progress of couples in the first few years of marriage is practically a waste of time. But it also

TABLE 1

*Proportion of Total Children in Family Borne by Specified Durations of Marriage England and Wales*

| Number of Years Married | All ages at Marriage Married in | | | Age of Mother at Marriage | | | | | | | | |
| | | | | Under 20 Married in | | | 20–24 Married in | | | 25–29 Married in | | |
| | 1929 | 1939 | 1949 | 1929 | 1939 | 1949 | 1929 | 1939 | 1949 | 1929 | 1939 | 1949 |
|---|---|---|---|---|---|---|---|---|---|---|---|---|
| 1 | 0·18 | 0·12 | 0·15 | 0·19 | 0·14 | 0·15 | 0·17 | 0·11 | 0·14 | 0·16 | 0·12 | 0·16 |
| 2 | 0·30 | 0·23 | 0·29 | 0·28 | 0·22 | 0·27 | 0·30 | 0·21 | 0·28 | 0·30 | 0·23 | 0·31 |
| 3 | 0·39 | 0·32 | 0·39 | 0·35 | 0·31 | 0·36 | 0·38 | 0·30 | 0·38 | 0·41 | 0·33 | 0·42 |
| 4 | 0·47 | 0·40 | 0·48 | 0·41 | 0·37 | 0·44 | 0·46 | 0·38 | 0·47 | 0·50 | 0·43 | 0·52 |
| 5 | 0·54 | 0·48 | 0·56 | 0·47 | 0·43 | 0·51 | 0·53 | 0·47 | 0·55 | 0·58 | 0·52 | 0·62 |
| 6 | 0·61 | 0·56 | 0·64 | 0·52 | 0·50 | 0·58 | 0·59 | 0·54 | 0·63 | 0·66 | 0·60 | 0·69 |
| 11 | 0·83 | 0·85 | 0·88 | 0·73 | 0·74 | 0·81 | 0·81 | 0·85 | 0·87 | 0·88 | 0·91 | 0·93 |
| 16 | 0·94 | 0·95 | 0·96 | 0·86 | 0·91 | 0·90 | 0·94 | 0·96 | 0·98 | 0·98 | 0·99 | 0·99 |
| 21 | 0·99 | 1·00 | 1·00 | 0·97 | 0·98 | 0·99 | 1·00 | 1·00 | 1·00 | 1·00 | 1·00 | 1·00 |
| 26 | 1·00 | 1·00 | 1·00 | 1·00 | 1·00 | 1·00 | 1·00 | 1·00 | 1·00 | 1·00 | 1·00 | 1·00 |

From P. R. Cox, 'Patterns and trends in recent British Population Developments', in *Biological Aspects of Social Problems*, Oliver & Boyd (1965).

shows, usefully, that 80% of children are born in the first ten years of marriage, so some general estimates of fertility are possible.

Information now exists too about the date of birth of each individual liveborn child so that the process of family building can be charted, but the *spacing* of births still needs to be recorded.

## THE QUALITY OF WILLINGNESS

What lies behind the bald facts on the waxing and waning of fertility? Most familiar generalizations trotted out in the past have proved to be wrong; indeed the statistical prophecies of the last 50 years have been distinguishable largely by their errors and not by their accuracies. For instance in rich countries like Britain and America, it used to be said that it was the wealthier, more educated, more urbanized communities which most reduced their fertility. Although this was true in the not so distant past it is these very people who are now starting to have larger families than the uneducated.

Darlington has recently put forward an argument which might help to explain the fall and then the rise in the birth rates of the higher classes, based on the 'willingness to have children'. If the quality of willingness is to some extent inherited, parents who wanted children would be selectively favoured. Thus after an initial fall in the birth-rate due to the effective use of contraceptive techniques the birth-rate would recover as the proportion of 'willing' people in the population increased. The argument has received some support by data reviewed by Carter, from Northwest Europe and North America where the birth rates in the upper classes have been on the increase during the last 20 years. However we are still very ignorant of the motives behind the facade of statistics, which make people willing to face the hardships and inconveniences of rearing a large family. Indeed fertility patterns go to the grass roots of human behaviour and human belief and our ignorance about these matters is great. Fertility seems to be related to cultural traditions, family organization, and economic needs, marriage practices, sexual behaviour and most important, religious conviction. This latter is often a powerful motive in regulating family size.

## DEATH

Turning now to statistics on mortality, these are based on the entries on death certificates which record the cause of death. Information is also obtained at registration of death on the sex, age and profession of the dead person. Such combined data can be used for many things to do with public health; to discover the proneness or not of various trades and professions to certain diseases and to link them with age of death. Sandblasters, for example, do not on average live as long as teachers; and doctors too, are shorter lived than teachers. Publicans, not surprisingly are top of the list for deaths from cirrhosis of the liver, often caused by excessive drinking. In spite of the many limitations imposed by the varying degree of ability of doctors, the accuracy and conscientiousness of doctors' entries and the changing fashions of medicine, death certificates have been a useful guide to the broad patterns and trends of a country's health. Table 2 shows that below the age of 55, death rates for men in England and Wales have been slightly reduced over the past 35 years. Over 55 no comparable improvement

### TABLE 2

*Death Rates by Sex and Age (per 1,000)*
*England and Wales*

|  | Men | | | | Women | | | |
|---|---|---|---|---|---|---|---|---|
|  | *35–44* | *45–54* | *55–64* | *65–74* | *35–44* | *45–54* | *55–64* | *65–74* |
| 1926–30 | 6·2 | 11·6 | 24·4 | 58·3 | 4·7 | 8·4 | 18·0 | 44·4 |
| 1936–40 | 5·0 | 11·0 | 25·0 | 56·8 | 3·8 | 7·5 | 16·5 | 41·8 |
| 1946–50 | 3·2 | 8·6 | 22·4 | 51·6 | 2·6 | 5·5 | 12·8 | 34·4 |
| 1956–60 | 2·4 | 7·4 | 21·9 | 53·7 | 1·8 | 4·5 | 10·9 | 30·7 |

From P. R. Cox, 'Patterns and trends in recent British Population Developments' in *Biological Aspects of Social Problems*, Oliver Boyd (1955).

is found. On this matter Sir Austin Bradford Hill and Professor Doll uttered the following chilly words: 'one of the most striking characteristics of British mortality in the last half century has been the lack of improvement in the death rate of men in middle life. Cigarette smoking may be one prominent cause.' This issue will be examined further in Chapter 20 but the statement is mainly based on a direct association between the number of cigarettes smoked and the chances of death from cancer of the lung, chronic bronchitis and coronary thrombosis.

# 3: The Fallibility of Statistics

IN 1935 Alexis Carell published a best-selling book, *Man—The Unknown*. Today, more than 30 years later we are still largely ignorant about large tracts of human natural history. The last chapter is based on data from a country with a high standard of vital statistics systems. But what of the availability of population 'facts' from poor countries?

In these countries data are often dependent on the accurate recall of a short-lived and illiterate people, prone to exaggeration and lapse of memory. Examination of population data from source books reveals a gross ignorance. In fact the base-line of fact on such matters as birth-rate, infant mortality and death-rate is not a line at all but a series of dots and dashes with wide gaps in it. In the census statistics of 1955–63, for example, 61 out of 229 countries, accounting for about a third of the world's population did not know their population size. There are still 34 countries and territories who have never taken a national population census—a universal count of the inhabitants of a certain well delimited territory at a specific time. Indeed those figures that are available might be incomplete or inflated and, because the methods used in the census vary from country to country, they must be used with caution in making inter-country comparisons.

NHM—C

Crude birth-rates do provide, as we have noted, a measure of gross additions to a population and, in combination with crude death rates, some estimate of population growth rates can be measured. The trouble with much of this information is the time lag between a birth and its registration. When a large proportion of live-birth registrations are delayed as in some parts of Latin-America, Asia and Africa, a very distorted picture of birth trends is produced. Examination of evidence from the U.S.A., Costa Rica, Chile and the Dominican Republic, to name a few countries, shows that delays of up to twenty to twenty-five years are not uncommon for birth registration, though the majority are recorded between two and four years of age. Current registration, therefore, is often masked by the inclusion of births that have taken place years before and a false picture of fertility is given. Nevertheless a general picture of fertility trends can be drawn providing it is realized that variation is great. In Africa, in Guinea, Mali and Niger for example, birth-rates are 55–60 per 1,000 of the population. In other parts, Zanzibar, Mauritania and Basutoland they are lower, at 40 per 1,000. In North America and Europe birth-rates are 25 per 1,000 or below and in some countries as low as 13 or 14 per 1,000.

To turn to another example. Classification of a population by age and sex is probably one of the most important items in population statistics. We have noted some of its uses in Fig. 7. But it throws light too on the manpower available to a country; it helps to forecast its school needs, its housing and food requirements and, as we have noted, its potential fertility. Yet in 1960 for only about half the world's population was it possible to obtain age/sex distribution figures for single years of age (although the five-year group distribution is available for 128 countries out of a total of 229). Single age measurements are useful to have for schooling, for example and many other necessities that cut across the five-year grouping. As expected, Africa is particularly lacking in data; only eight per cent of the population has its age/sex distribution recorded in single years. There are holes too in data from South America, Europe and Asia where the coverage is 10%, 47% and 50% respectively. In North America 78% of the population is covered. Even for the five-year age grouping Africa is again the dark continent with only 20 of its 59 countries and territories, or 37% of its population represented. But South America is worse. Here current age/sex data is available for only a quarter of the continent. Such data are available for half of Asia's population and two thirds of that of Europe. Poor coverage indeed, for such vital information about ourselves. The quality of the available data is often suspect too; age is often exaggerated and dates of birth forgotten. The problem is that illiterate people simply do not care and in answer to census questions will say anything or deliberately lie. The data collected often reveal a tendency to state ages in certain digits ending in 0,2,5 and 8. Number 13 is avoided!

The limitations of mortality statistics in England and Wales have been mentioned and will be expounded in Chapter 18. What of the poor regions of the world like Asia and South America? Here, doctors (and hospital beds) are few and far between. A few figures for comparison will underline this point. In the U.S.S.R. there are 310 inhabitants per doctor, in the U.S.A. 780, in Brazil 2,100, in India 2,400, in Nigeria 32,000 and in Niger 103,000. Distribution of qualified doctors is revealing too. As expected, most of them live and work in cities but most of the population is rural. In South America 20% of the population is urban and over half the doctors work in cities. The ratio of doctors in rural areas varies from 0·5 to 8·0 per 10,000 of the population.

In Madras (1953) there were only 0·38 hospital beds per 1,000 births in rural areas compared with 1·4 in the urban areas. In Bombay State differences were greater: 0·055 and 1·2 per 100 births in the rural and urban areas respectively. In India as a whole general hospital beds, medical officers and sanitary inspectors were maldistributed between rural and urban areas. In 1956 in rural areas the population per hospital bed was 8,050, in urban areas 579; population per medical officer was 49,763 in rural areas, 23,096 for urban areas and population per sanitary or health inspector in rural areas was 137,293 compared with 40,712 for urban areas. It is obvious that data on the age and cause of death in regions like Africa, Asia and South America are not worth a candle. Death certificates often record an unknown cause of death ('fevers of unknown origin' account for most deaths in developing countries) or else the cause is entered by a layman and has no meaning. Comparisons of causes of death from country to country can therefore be most misleading. It is worth noting too that comparison of the incidence of disease is made, not between different *races* but between country and country. Comparison between races might be equally important in helping to sort out the genetical basis of disease.

Of course deaths often go unreported in poorer countries. As far as infant deaths are concerned (long regarded as a useful measure of health) registration is often not made, especially if a baby dies in the first few days of life. Omissions are commoner in rural areas where unconventional disposal of the body is easier than in towns.

Enough has been said to show that much simple information needs to be gathered about man. To be sure it is easier said than done. Even the best oiled statistical machine would develop a knock when faced with the job of recording the masses in the shanties and on the pavements of the near urban slums in Asia. Not only in Asia, Africa and Latin America but in London, Paris and New York do the urban masses huddle yearly closer together.

Population statistics have been discussed at some length because they are the basis of the study of man's natural history. The statistics may seem dry but in these figures one can see the changing patterns and problems of living societies.

# Part 2: The Amateur of the Animal Kingdom

Part 2: The Amateur of the
Animal Kingdom

# 4: Nature and Nurture

## INTRODUCTION

VITAL statistics help in a rough way to map the patchy distribution of man and, with imagination, help to fill in some of the natural history of people in different countries: their average length of life, their wanderings, their many languages and what they die of. Two other problems we need to explore to find out more about man as an animal are: that of 'nature and nurture', and 'homeostasis'. Both will help us to get *inside* the human animal and observe him from another dimension.

In crude terms the nature/nurture question asks, 'How much part does the environment play in moulding the characteristics of the individual?' Homeostasis is a concept which helps to answer the question, 'How does the body manage to buffer itself against surroundings that may be continually changing and tending to destroy it?' How, for instance, do men on an overland expedition adjust to change in heat, cold, altitude, different foods and so on? An explanation of both concepts brings us to the world of the genes, lying beyond the microscope.

## NATURE AND NURTURE

In any large city we constantly meet people from different lands. A turbaned Sikh far away from his home in Northern India, with dark eyes and beard, a Yoruba from Nigeria with tightly coiled black hair, black skin and eyes and protruding lips. Whether in Timbuctoo or Birmingham these characteristics remain toughly persistent. No amount of sun, wind or different food will alter them. Then we might meet a friend, tanned after a holiday in Spain. In a crude way these illustrate nature and nurture. The differences between the Sikh, the man from Nigeria and the Englishman represent differences in ancestry. Each has come from parents of the same mould as himself and the mould faithfully reproduces in him all the racial features of his past. The tenacity with which these traits stick from generation to generation is called heredity (nature). A companion volume to this book* describes the way heredity works. All we need say here is that the chromosomes have the main say in heredity and the genes which are lodged on the chromosomes in the fertilized egg provide the blueprint from which the child develops. A gene is not a miniature eye, ear lobe, heart, brain etc. ready to grow into the adult form of the organ. It is a complex chemical which provides the organism with a specific capacity for performance. As soon as the egg is fertilized in the womb the heredity of the child is fixed. Nothing can alter it. Half the heredity will have come from the mother through the chromosomes in her egg, half from the father carried in his sperm. The fertilized egg carries 46 chromosomes (23 from each parent) with perhaps 10,000 gene pairs carried on the chromosome set. Often the genetic blueprint of the child is slightly different from that contributed by each parent. This is because the bits of heredity, the genes, can be combined and recombined in different ways, during reproduction. Although all the genes may well be the same as those of the parents, they may be arranged in a slightly different *order* on the chromosomes, and this may give a different effect in the offspring. Sometimes however a gene might be quite different from that of the parent. It has altered its nature or *mutated*. The gene rearrangements and the occasional mutations help to make us differ from our parents, however slightly. As will be now clear, each of us has been formed by a sort of genetic lottery; we are but *one* of a vast consort of 'possible children', any of whom might have been conceived and born if a different sperm with its different gene

* *Biology and the Social Crisis* (Heinemann Educational Books, 1967).

arrangements had chanced to fertilize the mother's egg cell, likewise with its different gene arrangements. The Sikh may have a different eye colour from that of his mother but his father's mouth, but basically his blueprint (and that of his possible brothers) which his parents provided him with, carried 'Sikh' instructions and it would be impossible for him to develop into an Englishman no matter how much beer, beef, and bread and cheese he is fed on. The environment cannot alter his natural characteristics, cannot change his heredity. Our sunburnt friend is another matter. It is a question of the kind of environment he has been in. Similarly his accent depends upon his family, his school, the company he keeps. It is changeable; the result of upbringing. But not entirely; and here is where we must avoid over-simplification. The sunburn depends upon a *potentiality* to sunburn and the quality and range of the voice depends on the characters of the structures producing the voice which are inherited through the genes.

Much has been learned in recent years about the hereditary basis of man's individuality. In most respects our properties and personalities are limited and prescribed by the genetic character of the fertilized egg; the rate and duration of our growth, our build, our hormone system and hence our temperaments and social habits. Also influenced are our educability; the structures producing our voice; our food requirements; our proneness to all the diseases that flesh is heir to and of course our sex, our fertility or sterility.

How then does nature react with nurture? Environment does sometimes stop the genetical potential from showing. Indeed it sometimes kills, especially at the infant stage in poor countries. And, as we shall see in Chapter 17 life has been extended in the United Kingdom from forty years a century ago to about seventy now. Better social conditions and medical treatment, in other words a better *nurture*, are allowing us to reach old age. Then, a home devoid of books or good conversation can stifle an average child's potential and hinder his progress although the brilliant child will hack his way out.

But let us take another tack. If our tanned Englishman was transplanted minus medical kit, to Western Nigeria beside the Yoruba who would live longer? Probably the Yoruba because his companion might well die from malaria or yellow fever, diseases which the Yoruba has the inherited capacity to resist. If the same pair went to the Andes with their wives and settled at an altitude of 14,000 feet would they be able to reproduce? They might, but the chances are that the ability of a foreign woman to shift enough oxygen from the oxygen-thin air of the mountains to the baby in the womb, is limited; and often the baby is lost through this incapacity of the heart, lungs and blood to shift enough oxygen to the baby. A native woman has all the right inborn adaptations to cope. These are rather crude examples of the interplay of nature and nurture. However the problem is much subtler than this, especially in relation to human behaviour.

One theory is that men choose instinctively or are chosen, by environments that fit them in body* and mind. The muscular extrovert is more often found in occupations that involve some rough and tumble, the Army or in physical education, than the beanpole-shaped introvert who is more often found in 'quieter' jobs, on the research side of a factory for example. Scrooge and Pickwick, Laurel and Hardy could hardly have had the same shapes but with behaviour swapped round; the characters seem to fit the body. And often the body with its personality, slots into the right groove in the environment.

We can learn something about this idea from animal studies. Davenport, an American zoologist at the turn of the century, noticed that each animal on a beach sought and selected the place in the environment that suited it best and the environment in its turn selected the most appropriate organisms. This natural, or 'double selection' must increase the speed of adaptive processes and be selected for in evolution. Animals, because they can move, choose the environment that fits them best, for camouflaging them for example, but the process supports the illusion that individuals are 'shaped and moulded' by the environment which in fact the animals have actively and instinctively chosen. Now, considering man, it is a gross oversimplification to say that men 'respond' to the environment like a plant thrusting to the light. The majority live in environments that have been created for them by their own type, in other words by people with their own kind of heredity. We shall return to this notion in Chapter 11 when we consider the biological origins of the class system; but the lines of the old hymn 'the rich man in his castle, the poor man at his gate, God made them high and lowly, he ordered their estate' have some truth. Let us pursue this a little further with a familiar example noted by C. D. Darlington. He wrote: 'we see different people sitting side by side in the same railway compartment. But they are living in different environments, for on the one hand they are reading different papers; and on the other hand they do not intend, or expect, or desire, to speak to one another. In urban societies, our lives are largely made up of such situations. They may be

* See *Biology and the Social Crisis*.

summed up by saying that we are engaged in choosing, and being chosen by, environments that fit us in body and mind.'

The social environment of man is a diversity of environments created by a diversity of heredities. Effort and choice by people are necessary only if environments are different (either better or worse), from those their parents gave them. Most human beings slip most easily into the environment created by their forebears.

## POPULATIONS AND EVOLUTION

We have put forward some ideas about the complex interactions of heredity and environment very much at the level of the individual. If a *population* of English people had gone to Tibet a few of them might have been able to resist the stresses of altitude and have been able to reproduce and maintain a population. It is the diverse genetic constitutions of men, which in the teeth of the powerful stresses of climate, altitude and disease have allowed certain of the migrating and conquering peoples to stand up to the new conditions and maintain a population. This is a theme which is developed in Chapter 8. If human populations had identical genetic outfits and thus formed a kind of genetic clone, the adaptive potential of men would be nil. The populations would neither have the genetic reserves to cope with a diverse environment nor would their descendants be fitted to survive in a changing world. Like timber that has no give, it would be splintered by the stress of change.

We shall deal with the origins of man in the next chapter, but the great strength of man compared with all other animals has been his retention of the *amateur status*. All other animals have in the course of evolution, become better and better adapted to a specialized type of environment. They are the professionals of their own niche. Witness the climatic adaptations of the polar bear in the Arctic, camels and fat-tailed sheep to the drought of deserts, water buffaloes in the tropics and the llamas, yaks and Bolivian geese of high altitudes whose blood has the capacity to soak up the scarce oxygen of high mountain air. Those animals that have failed to fit into this lock and key situation have been wiped out. Man is uncommitted. As we shall see in Chapter 5, not only is he capable of withstanding fluctuations in heat, cold and altitude but he can become immune to many diseases and cope with an enormous range of foods. He is able to interbreed, black with white, yellow with brown, and produce normal offspring, for man's genetic outfit, his genes and chromosomes, are the common property of the whole human species. Although it is true and obvious that genetic group differences do exist to give racial variations, they are not different enough to make breeding between the groups impossible. Of the 20,000* or so genes attributed to man, it has been tentatively suggested that 90–99% are held in common by all groups of men. Of the remaining 1–10% most might be responsible for racial variations in physiology, growth rate, adult body form, differences between male and female, and many other submerged features like disease resistance†. This characteristic of interbreeding does not apply even to the most closely related species of animal. Under natural conditions, closely related species do not mate, for their food preferences, territories and behaviour do not overlap. If they do mate, there is no offspring, or the offspring is sterile. The offspring may live because the genetic blueprints of the parents produce together a viable plan. But the hybrid's own reproductive organs and its own sperm or eggs carry a faulty blueprint so the hybrid is sterile. The behavioural or territorial barrier to cross-breeding between closely-related species is there for good reason; to preserve the genetic identity of the species. If this identity were destroyed by cross-breeding and the bits of heredity were combined in new ways, then the offspring would no longer be closely adapted to their conditions of life; and close adaptation is necessary for survival.

Man himself, in the long past, must have begun to differentiate into distinct sub-species, each accumulating its own distinctive genetic constitution. But migration and conquest followed by cross-breeding, mixed up the sub-species before each had crossed the genetic brink to full speciation. In spite of this, different peoples have special 'adaptations' to their environments. These adaptations are embedded in a general flexibility which allows man to live in a wide range of environments.

* The true figure is probably not less than 2,000 or more than 50,000. Twenty thousand is an arbitrary figure given by Stern, in *Principles of Human Genetics*.

† It should be emphasized that characters like fertility, physique or 'intelligence' are under the control of many genes each having a small effect and may be subject to marked environmental influence. As yet we have no reliable estimate of the number of the 'polygenes' involved, their interaction with one another or their interaction with environmental influences.

# 5: Homeostasis

THE adaptability of man and other mammals (and birds) is based on homeostatic or self-regulating mechanisms. Indeed the general ability of living things to maintain their own constancy has impressed biologists throughout the ages. The survival of any organism depends very largely on its ability to neutralize or repair the disturbances that are produced in it by its surroundings. The more advanced the creature the more perfect and complex do these self-regulating mechanisms become. By a strange paradox man and other mammals can only maintain their stability because they *are* excitable, capable of modifying themselves according to external stimuli and adjusting their responses to the degree of stimulation. As W. B. Cannon wrote of the human body, '. . . in a sense it is stable because it is modifiable'.

To keep the machinery of the body working smoothly, there are certain corrective agencies which in the main, act through a special part of the nervous system which functions as a regulating mechanism. These corrective agencies are there to maintain the 'internal environment' of the body within very narrow limits from which deviation would be dangerous. Water content, salt concentration, sugar, fat and protein levels in the blood are held in balance. Together with oxygen supply to the body and body temperature these substances are monitored very carefully by the alert sentinels of the body—the nerve endings. Two of the outposts of the body where these nerve endings exist are the mouth and stomach. Dryness of the mouth sends us in search of water and hunger makes us hunt for food. In satisfying thirst and hunger the internal conditions of the body are held in balance, and the efficiency of the system is remarkable. A man can survive dry heat temperatures up to 128°F *without* an increase in body temperature above normal (98·4°F).

The importance of maintaining this internal balance within fine limits lies in the protection of the fragile chemical systems of the body which work within a limited range of temperature, acidity and oxygen supply. Because they are so rigorously guarded any man, no matter what his colour is, can survive in a wide range of environments, heat and cold, dry and wet, high and low.

The protective advantage of this internal stability is much more important than economy. To preserve balance the body will get rid of water, salts and sugar by sweating or in the urine, if they are present in excess. A beautiful example of conservation processes is that of starvation. The first reserve to go is glycogen, then fat, then protein. First, the least essential organs (the gluteal muscles for example) lose the reserves and the heart and brain are the last. In fact death occurs usually before heart and brain become protein donors at all.

Sometimes the body is driven to violent measures to preserve the constancy of the internal environment. Violent shivering helps to produce extra heat and so prevent a fall in body temperature; convulsions brought on by low blood sugar content, stimulate the production of hormones which cause extra sugar to be released from liver glycogen and so preserve sugar balance. But these violent measures are seldom necessary; milder processes suffice. However they are there in reserve to maintain balance in times of emergency.

Extra evidence which strengthens the notion that 'stability is more important than economy' is supplied by the fact that vital organs like the heart are not built on a pinched and skimpy scale but with enormous inbuilt safety factors. The heart usually beats moderately about seventy times a minute, pushing out a moderate volume of blood. But at any moment it is ready to contract twice as fast and push out twice as much blood per beat. Most bodily organs come in pairs too and this is protective. Life can continue even though a large part of the lungs have been destroyed. All this evidence and much more shows that just as an engineer would multiply his estimates of load, pressure and so forth by five or ten, so the body is built to take extra strain to maintain homeostasis.

From what was said earlier, it is clear that homeostasis depends on the genetic constitution of the individual and the population of which he is part. We know that the human species have most of their genes in common and common homeostatic properties. Because of the pile-up of genes here and there, giving this or that adaptation, certain populations will have different homeostatic properties. The Eskimo will differ from the Dinka who herds his cattle under the hot sun in the deserts of the Upper Nile; the South American Indian of the high Andes will differ from the Pygmy of the tropical rain forests of the Congo. But any population be it Dinka, Eskimo, Indian or Chinese will contain a spread of individuals, some more adapted than others in homeostatic properties—most will cluster about a mean value.

We must not forget that *cultural* practices are homeostatic. They may act as a shield under which man can survive and breed with a genetic endowment, which, in the absence of culture, would not allow him to survive. Houses, clothes, fire, medicine, surgery, canned food, can make up for his deficiencies, to keep him in balance with his environment. And what is not often realized, cultural practices can protect the group against the deviant individual whose behaviour is outside the permitted range. We know from certain case histories that among peoples hard pressed for food, like the Central Eskimos and the Australian aborigines of the Western Desert of Australia, trouble makers are killed. If the cause of their anti-social behaviour is inherited and they are got rid of before they can reproduce, their genes will have no chance of being passed on to the next generation. The standard of social graces required by Western society acts as an optimum value controlling for example how we use a knife and fork, and discourages us from such habits as picking our nose in public. Deviants are cold-shouldered. If they find this disagreeable they might conform to group behaviour. If they do not they might be ostracized to such a degree that they fail to get a mate and thus their genetic potential is lost. Cultural practices and rituals bind societies together to maintain their integrity. In other words they maintain the homeostasis of the group.

Finally we might ask, 'What is the significance of homeostasis apart from its enabling us to exploit a wide range of environments?' This in-built quality we now realize allows people to go anywhere in the world. In the past it allowed peoples to migrate to strange lands and conquer foreign people, put up with different foods and ward off strange diseases. We shall examine migration further in chapters 24 to 30, but apart from this, homeostasis allows us to be freed from the worry about the working of our insides and we can use our brain for more important social and creative jobs.

# Part 3: Man's Past as an Introduction to Man Now

# 6: The Life and Times
# of Early Man

## TIME SCALES AND SNAGS

FORTY thousand generations ago in Africa a population of man-like apes were turning into ape-like men. This population must have been more than a few hundred because otherwise it would have been too small to provide a sufficient supply of heritable variation for natural selection to bring about the evolutionary changes it has since that time. It must have been of the order of 10,000 or 100,000 but it is from such a genetically diverse population that man evolved and from no Adam and Eve. Set against life as a whole, man's evolution from the man-apes is short probably of the order of one or two million years.[*] Life in some form has probably existed for at least 2,000 million years; so the *proportion* of the total time scale occupied by the ape-men and their successors up to ourselves is about $\frac{1}{2000}$th of it. Modern, civilized man of course takes up a far, far smaller proportion of time. To put into perspective the place of man on earth imagine a thick book of some 6,000 pages and assign to each page a million years,

[*]Evidence of the existence of Australopithecus three or four million years ago has been found in the Omo valley in Ethiopia.

since the earth is said to be about 6,000 million years old. The first 4,000 pages of our book would be blank. Then the first traces of life would appear in the sea, then on the land, recording the slow and painful story of invertebrate to vertebrate, fish to mammal, mammal to man. Only at page 5,998 or 5,999 would the story of man come to be written and only on the last two or three lines of the last page would modern man come on the scene.

The mechanism of natural selection which changed man from what he was to what he is now and what he will be (and this includes not only changes in form and physique but changes in temperament, intelligence and morals) will not be described here. Sufficient to say that it is based on the ruthless, automatic pruning process which eliminates the less 'efficient' variants in a population, leaving the organisms most adapted to their conditions of life to survive and reproduce. As we have learned in Chapter 4 the course of animal evolution is directed partly by the external environment and partly by the choice of appropriate environment by the animal. Very early man was, no doubt, like animals in this respect and probably the evolution of the human *races* was largely directed by the external habitat.* But on the other hand, man's *internal character* based on his brain was probably the agent of the directed change which controlled the later evolution of the species. In other words the races and the species may have evolved by different methods; the former largely animal like, based in the main on the stresses of the environment with this doing the picking and choosing, the latter based on the evolution of the brain.

Fig. 10 shows the immediate forebears of man stretching back across a million years. It is as well to be slightly sceptical of such charts for they make human evolution look like a straightforward chain of events. Such diagrams have been constructed from bits of bones, a foot, a piece of charcoal, found perhaps on the floor of a cave where, by chance they have been preserved. Dating these relics is difficult because as someone once wrote, fossils are not found with labels on them and in spite of modern tests there is still a good deal of uncertainty about the age of fossils. Then, because a few skulls and teeth of man-ape have been dug up in South Africa, it does not necessarily mean that the birthplace of early man was there. The richness of man-ape finds here may be due to the presence of limestone caves that made good fossil traps. It may be that the man-apes lived widely in the Old World and

* See *Biology and the Social Crisis* for an account of natural selection in man.

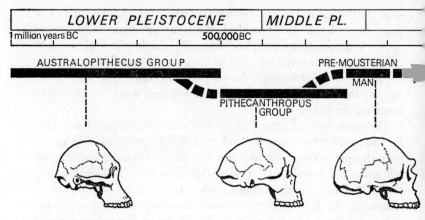

FIG. 10 A time chart of the immediate forebears of modern man during the last million years with outlines of the skulls of the principal fossil types. Each group, here represented by a single broad line, is made up of a number of different fossil forms, some of which, especially in the Australopithecus and Pithecanthropus (Homo erectus) groups, are given distinct specific or even generic rank by different experts; each group may be a branching system of at

traces of them have yet to be discovered. So, although these diagrams with neat successions of climate, advancement of tools and enlarging brain cases are useful and necessary, it is as well to remember that they have been constructed from scattered bits of data.

## THE LIFE AND TIMES OF AUSTRALOPITHECUS AND HOMO ERECTUS

The earliest fossil forms of man ape have been found in East Africa. They are those of *Australopithecus* of which perhaps about 100 individuals are known in the fossil history and which date from a time between two million and half a million years ago. These man-apes were clever, erect, two-footed creatures who made tools from split or trimmed pebbles perhaps to cut up small animals for food (see Plate I*a*). They probably used bone tools as well, the teeth-lined jaws of antelopes for scraping, but in general none of the tools was big enough to cut up a large animal. They had reduced canines and indeed almost human teeth but in this respect (and no doubt others) they were variable. Some of the ape-men population had heavy jaws and massive teeth probably

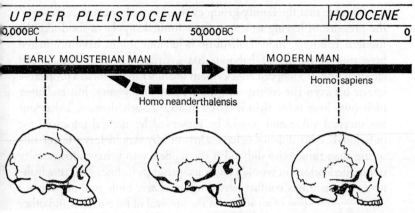

least different races, and perhaps some distinct species, but our knowledge is not yet sufficient to justify the charting of what are still hypothetical details. The point of origin of Neanderthal man is disputed. The outlines of the skulls representing each group, are drawn to the same scale. After Hardy, *The Living Stream*, Collins, 1965.

to help them chew plant food—others were light-jawed and probably fed on a mixed diet. Only his cunning and his ability to use tools saved *Australopithecus* from his enemies for he was slow-moving and his teeth were not strong enough to defend himself with.

Perhaps these shadowy figures of the long past had a stable and well-adapted social organization, rather like the present day baboons of Ethiopia. Of course we are forced to speculate here for the behaviour of our ancestors a million years ago leaves no trace, like their skeletons. But comparisons of present-day species of animals can give deep insight into the evolutionary history of our own species. The study of baboons for example has shown that they form family groups of one male, one or two females and their young. Such groupings seem to be an adaptive response to exploit a sparse and scattered source of food from a wide area over which the families range. The family groups band together as troupes of fifty or more animals at a time and in larger groups of seven hundred or more for sleeping and protection.

*Australopithecus*, like the baboons, probably evolved in country where food was scattered and in short supply rather like the hills, valleys and treeless flats of parts of South Africa today where antelopes, hyenas, lions and baboons still roam. Although it may appear to be far-fetched it is possible that the family group evolved in early man in response to the pressure of having to search for a limited supply of food like the modern baboons. Indeed altruistic behaviour might have originated here too. A troupe of baboons has a firm principle: women and children first. If a leopard attacks them the older males form a protective screen between the enemy and the females and young, but endanger their own lives more than if they ran away. Such altruistic behaviour has survival value and would be preserved by natural selection, for individuals who did not behave altruistically would leave fewer off-spring than those who did and if the tendency to behave altruistically is inherited, selection would favour its spread. Selfishness and unselfishness, representing a conflict between the relative biological importance of self-preservation of an adult and the survival of his children and other members of the family group, has a long history.

*Homo erectus* (*Pithecanthropus*), the earliest form of ape-like man, was in existence in South Africa about a million years ago and later fossil forms of him have been found in North Africa, Java, China and Germany. He was an ape-man with the accent on man. He had acute senses, great intelligence and manipulating ability. He used clubs of wood and bone and perhaps slings (see Plate I*b*).

## THE PRINCIPLE OF SELF-EXAGGERATION

Such inventions as slings must depend on a high degree of muscular, skeletal, nervous and mental organization. The very use of such weapons must have swung open the doors to allow greater brain growth. It is possible that each invention (tools, weapons, shelters) was due to hereditary abilities *and each invention gave greater advantage to more ability of a similar kind*. This theory of self-exaggerating effect with a positive feed back may have led to continual change in one direction. It is well known in the evolution of the foot of the horse and in the elephant's trunk, and here we see it applied to man's brain, which has changed gradually in one direction over a great period of time, perhaps over half a million years or 20,000 generations (see Plate 2*a*, *b*, *c*). This 'directed' evolution of the brain may have been set in motion when, with each advance in his intelligence, his former methods of defence by tooth and claw declined and made him *more* dependent on his intelligence. The races, isolated from one another, were thus bound to change in the same direction in parallel with one another. As each

**Plate 1a.** AUSTRALOPITHECUS. The earliest hominids lived in open country, obtaining meat by scavenging and by hunting small or young animals. Even in males the eye-teeth were small and level with the grinders (molars). From a painting by M. Wilson.

t is as well to remember that these aintings are imaginative reconstrucions from the data of bits of bone and few teeth (see Plate 2).

**Plate 1b.** *Homo erectus.* Remains of Java Man have been found in river gravels at Trinil and at Sangiran. M. Wilson.

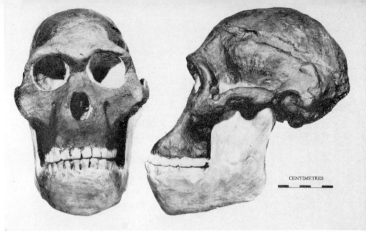

**Plate 2a.** Model of restored skull of *Autralopithecus* from cave deposit at Sterkfontein, Transvaal.

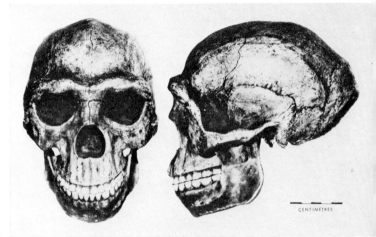

**Plate 2b.** Model of restored skull of Peking Man (*Homo erectus* from Peking) from cave deposit at Choukoutein, China.

**Plate 2c.** Skull of Cheddar Man (*Homo sapiens*) from Gough's Cave, Cheddar, Somerset.

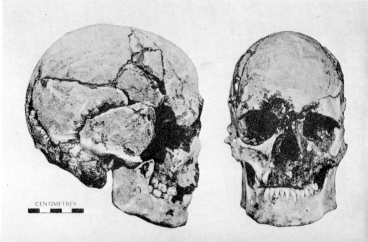

tool or weapon was invented it sharpened the selection against those who could not exploit it. The principle of self-exaggeration is with us today. Witness the countries who lag in the application of science to the problems of health and disease, agriculture and weapon development and at what a disadvantage they are as compared with the rich, powerful and science based countries. The old saying that money breeds money is an illustration of the principle.

It was not only the invention of tools that was important for directed evolution but hereditary ability of all kinds. But the important point is that man always came first with his diverse and inborn gifts and created culture. And by creating culture and altering the environment man gave himself something new to be selected for. This led in itself to the progressive character of human culture. As Gordon Childe wrote 'man makes himself'.

# 7: Man's First and Second Expansions

ERHAPS half a million years ago man's first great expansion
began across parts of Europe, Africa and Asia. Why? No doubt
there are many reasons, but climatic amelioration and the
development of speech must have been important ones. Let us take the
climatic reason a little further. Man appeared during the Pleistocene
period in geological history. This represents the last million years and
is the period of the ice age. But it was not one continuous period of intense cold. There was a succession of five major spells of cold broken by
four warmer ages and themselves varying by smaller oscillations.
During the cold periods, evaporation lowered the oceans to feed the
growing polar and alpine ice; islands such as Britain and Japan were
joined on to the continental mainlands and America and Asia were connected while the islands between Australia and Asia made an almost
continuous bridge. As the ice pushed out, it narrowed the living girdle
of the earth to the equatorial regions and within that girdle rainfall was
heavy, favouring equatorial forest. Then, during the warmer periods the
ice shrunk as it is doing now. Temperature rose, rainfall lessened and the
living girdle enlarged towards the poles. At other times the ice came

back. It was during this accordion-like action of the ice that the chance came for man to expand. On foot with only the dog, fire and stone tools to aid him man pushed out. The warm interglacials opened his path to the far North, up the Nile valley into Asia and Europe. No doubt, at times, he walked across land where seas now are. At any rate between 500,000 and 50,000 years ago man had spread his wide-meshed net or sparse population throughout the Old World. We can be no more certain of dates than this.

This first expansion of man is certainly one of the most remarkable or human achievements. When the ice retreated it needed men of a certain *type* to seize the chance to explore. Perhaps the invention of co-operative hunting, depending again on more brain power and more complex nervous and behavioural adaptations, helped. And speech may have developed well enough to plan a day's hunting so that a group of men could talk over, the night before, the morrow's plans. In this way, as Sears has reminded us, knowledge could be exchanged and accumulated and passed on down the generations, an immense breakthrough over the old 'do-it-yourself, learn-the-hard-way' system of nature. Man's ability to manipulate objects and store experience probably enabled him to get round the barriers of temperature, aridity, space, seas and mountains and barriers that have always restricted other species to specific inches.

## HOMO SAPIENS

Somewhere in the chunk of time between 500,000 and 250,000 years ago *Homo erectus* evolved into *Homo sapiens*, our own species.

How did *H. erectus* cross the boundary to the *sapiens* species? As Coon suggests, it is likely that it was the result of peripheral matings between members of neighbouring populations rather than several step-by-step mutations. And the change from one species to the other must have occurred at different times in different populations depending on which population got the new genetic trait first. This would depend on the proximity of populations and the strength of the mating barriers between them.

The races of *H. sapiens* became adapted to the regional differences in climate, altitude, disease and mode of life. They diverged most notably in skin colour, head shape and organs of speech. And going hand in hand with these were the self-exaggerating changes explained above, which led to general increases in intelligence and hence to the parallel evolution of the European, Mongolian and Negro peoples that are living today.

The earliest fossils of *Homo sapiens* come from Swanscombe in England and Stenheim in Germany. These subspecies of *Homo sapiens* lived about 200,000 years ago, Swanscombe man in woodlands bordering on the River Thames, during a warm interglacial period. His brain was bigger than that of *Homo erectus*—1,300 cc compared with 1,100 cc— but his face and jaws were heavy. In Europe he was replaced by Neanderthaloid man, also a subspecies of *H. sapiens*, about 75,000 years ago who was more primitive looking than the Swanscombe-Stenheim populations.

## NEANDERTHAL MAN

Neanderthal man had a stocky figure with short powerful legs and impressive forearms; his heavy face had a prow-like nose and a slant brow. Coon suggests that the beaky nose might have acted as a 'radiator' preventing the brain (which needs to be kept at a constant temperature) from being chilled by very cold air. Neanderthal man was typically a cave dweller. But although this sounds primitive in the extreme his stone implements were good and his brain size has not been beaten by modern man. He piously buried his dead, removing their heads and eating their brains, a custom which probably foreshadows the religious feeling of later peoples.

In later times, men like Neanderthal man occupied S.W. Asia and North Africa. He remained in Europe until about 40,000 years ago when he was snuffed out by modern forms of *Homo sapiens*. Perhaps 'snuffed out' gives the wrong impression—although in evolutionary time Neanderthal man might as well have been pushed over the edge of a cliff. In fact the replacement of Neanderthal man by Cro-Magnon man must have taken many centuries. It is likely that Neanderthal man was not merely exterminated but 'absorbed' by cross matings into the Cro-Magnon population. Indeed some of his cold-adapting genes might well have been useful to the survival of Cro-Magnon man particularly when the ice-sheets advanced once more. The distributions of early man from his emergence to about 40,000 years ago is shown in Fig. 11.

The sudden invasion of Europe by the new men showed that they

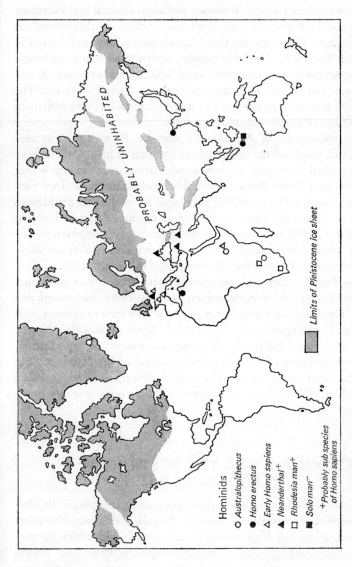

FIG. 11 Distribution of early man from his first appearance to about 40,000 years ago. After a map in *Man and his Environment*, B.B.C. 1964.

PROBABLY UNINHABITED

Hominids

○ Australopithecus
● Homo erectus
△ Early Homo sapiens
▲ Neanderthal[+]
□ Rhodesia man[+]
■ Solo man[−]

Limits of Pleistocene ice sheet

[+] Probably sub species of Homo sapiens

must have been evolving elsewhere and were the edge of a tide that had just reached Europe. Evidence points to Central and Northern Africa and Southern Asia as the evolutionary cauldrons that poured out the invaders. They were the Cro-Magnon men who were followed in Western Europe by Neolithic peoples, agriculturalists and herdsmen. This agricultural stage originated in the Middle East between 6000 and 7000 B.C. but started in Britain much later, around 3000 B.C. The Neolithic farmers were followed by waves of others carrying with them the cultures of the Bronze and Iron Ages.

The replacement of Neanderthal man by *Homo sapiens* around 40000 B.C., marks off the second great expansion of man. Outside Europe it pushed man outwards into South Africa, over the dry Bering Straights into North America probably (and estimates of dates vary greatly) about 20,000 or 30,000 years ago; across the Panama isthmus down to Tierra del Fuego by 7000 B.C. and into Australia between 15,000 and 20,000 years ago. The momentum of the expansion continued until quite recently when the Polynesians colonized New Zealand in A.D. 950 and the Eskimos Greenland in A.D. 1300.

Cro-Magnon man and his successors in Europe left tools that were clearly used for hunting, fishing, woodworking, basketwork and so on. These tools and weapons enabled the new men to conquer, colonize and open up new supplies of food. Again these skills enhanced those who could use them. They must have favoured, by selection, greater elaboration of nervous control, leading no doubt to increasing regional diversity in speech. Once again every invention, technical or intellectual, brought about a change in man's own character by its success.

## EXPANSION AND THE DESTRUCTION OF PLEISTOCENE FAUNA

One biological effect of these expansions may be mentioned: the destruction of the Pleistocene fauna mainly by palaeolithic man. This fauna is dominated by big, highly-adapted land animals with which big predators and scavengers are associated—huge elephants and rhinos, giraffes, vultures, storks, antelopes—and was present on all the continents, but only Africa has a characteristic Pleistocene Fauna today. Big elephants and rhinos were even present in the tundra with its permanently frozen sub-soil. In Europe and in most of Asia the Pleistocene fauna collapsed over 100,000 years ago, in North America about 8,000 years ago, in the West Indies and Central and Southern America rather later than this, in Australia, not more than 20,000 years ago and in New Zealand, after A.D. 950. James Fisher puts the collapse of the Pleistocene fauna (as characterized by its more exaggerated and highly adapted forms) down to the arrival on the scene of man the hunter: a hunter whose range of kill improved continually by invention of spear, trap, bolas, bow and arrow and a host of other devices.

As we have seen in Europe, for example, *Homo sapiens* was present about 200,000 years ago. As his skills improved the forest elephant and hippopotamus and perhaps the giant vulture vanished about 100,000 years ago. The forest rhino disappeared not long afterwards. In North America the extinction of the Pleistocene fauna was more sudden, in keeping with the sudden invasion and penetration of the continent by modern man. Of 54 different species of mammals fossilized in the la Brea tarpits of Los Angeles (dating from 18,000 to about 4,500 years ago) 24 are now extinct and of 113 fully identified birds, 22 are extinct. The huge dire wolf, the vast short-faced bear, the big sabre-toothed cat, the giant lion, the super-camel or super-llama (7 feet at the withers), the American Mastodon and others are all gone. It seems certain, Fisher writes, that they did not become extinct until after the coming of man–probably between 11,000 and 8,000 years ago, a period when man, according to archaeological evidence, must have been well established in North America.

How is it that the Pleistocene fauna has not vanished in Africa? It was in Africa that man evolved and so he had longer to kill. The paradox may be explained as follows. As man evolved in Africa, *the fauna evolved with him* and developed adaptations to defend itself. Probably palaeolithic man did destroy some large African species but he did not extinguish the Pleistocene fauna. It was only when man carrying all the know-how of killing skill, invaded new areas (like North America for example) that their faunas, which had not adapted to man, became extinct.

Stone Age man then was a fauna-exterminator. We shall see later in Chapter 15 that destruction of habitat accelerated in the Neolithic age.

# 8: Adaptation to Disease, Altitude and Climate

AS the second expansion went on climate and disease acted as selective sieves probably, allowing through only those populations who had the genetic variability to adapt. In looking at a few examples of local adaptations which probably arose during this expansion we must take as our unit of evolutionary measurement at least 100 human generations. One example will indicate the importance of genetic diversity. The Mongolian invaders of the New World found in North America climates like those they had left behind. But in South America, the men who had been sieved through the Arctic conditions of the Bering land bridge met new physiological challenges: foetid and seasonally flooded jungles, dry scrub-covered hills, the thin air of mountains. In less than 20,000 years, however, South America had been colonized and in this time man had adapted sufficiently to allow his survival both in the wet cold of Tierra del Fuego and the wet heat of the Amazon basin and from the driest deserts in the world to the highest mountains.

As man expanded over the world he must have faced new enemies in each region: insects, lice, worms, flukes, bacteria and viruses; often these were combined. The mosquito carried the malarial parasite and the flea carried the plague bacillus. Diseases then, must have been powerful agents of selection and among these malaria must take pride of place. It is, or has been, almost world wide and when it does not kill it weakens to the point of incompetence. Malaria itself may have been less of a burden to man in his food-gathering stages of economy but with the invention of agriculture, some 10,000 years ago, it became so. This is because primitive agricultural methods create places in which the mosquito larvae can mature—puddles, ditches and the like. The bi-product of agriculture, too, is greater density of people and accumulation of filth, catalysts to disease transmission.

In the last two millenia perhaps, various genetic shields have arisen in human populations inhabiting countries where one of the various forms of malaria is prevalent. One of these genetic defences is based on the production of blood pigments which are indigestible to the malarial parasite. It perhaps arose first in the Bantu people. Not only do these genes ward off malaria but they helped to protect these early populations from disturbance by less well-adapted peoples (those who carried no protective genes against malaria). Thus these genetic defences along with the geographical barriers of seas, mountains, rivers and deserts must have helped to maintain the backwardness found in many tropical populations. But a price has to be paid for the genetic defences. They have the disastrous effect of replacing energy by lethargy in the man or woman who carries them. As Darlington writes,'They turn the alert and free into the submissive and enslavable.' For these reasons disease may well have prevented Africa from developing. Until recent times it has destroyed or deterred all immigrants or invaders of Africa who did not breed with the native population and whose offspring would thus get a share of the protective genes. And tropical diseases due to protozoa and helminth worms (see Table 3) have no genetic resistance in man. It is highly possible that these tropical diseases crippled African societies just at the moment when their populations reached the numbers and densities necessary for civilization.

Climate and altitude too must have been stringent agents of selection and the success of the migrating peoples must have been proportionate to their genetic variability. The first effects of an environmental change are felt in the chemical machinery of the body when alterations in blood chemistry, in pigment development and fat storage take place. The alteration of these chemical processes may require anatomical

## TABLE 3

### Supposed Origins and Distributions of the Historic Diseases of Man

| | Climatically less Selective | | Climatically more Selective | |
|---|---|---|---|---|
| | Air-borne | Contact, Water, Soil | Animal Vectors | |
| OLD WORLD | V. Poliomyelitis (O.K.)<br>**Smallpox** (China)<br>**Measles** (Medit.)<br>Diphtheria (O.K.)<br>B. **Pneumonia** (O.K.) | B. Cholera (India)<br>Typhoid (unknown)<br>Gonorrhoea (O.K.)<br>Tetanus (Greece)<br><br>H. Trichinosis (pig: S.W. Asia)<br>Hookworm spp. (Africa) (warm climates) | *Temperate*<br>B. Typhus (Athens, 430 B.C.)<br>Plague (O.T.; Samuel)<br>*Tropical*<br>V. **Yellow Fever**† (W. Africa)<br>B. Leprosy (O.K.)<br>P. Encephalitis★ (Africa)<br>Malaria★ (Africa, c. 1000 B.C.)<br>H. Filariasis (tropics)<br>Bilharzia★ (O.K.) | lice<br>fleas<br><br>mosquito<br>fleas<br>tsetse<br>mosquito<br>mosquito<br>snail |
| NEW WORLD | — | B. **Syphilis** (to O./W. 1492) | *Tropical*<br>P. Encephalitis | lice |
| PALEOLITHIC | B. Tuberculosis (cold climates) | B. Yaws (fly-borne) | — | |

V. virus. B. bacteria, *Rickettsia* or spirochaete. P. protozoa. H. helminth. O.K. Old Kingdom, Egypt.

★ Deadly diseases of Africa for which no simple genetic resistance can be selected.

† Derived probably from African monkeys.

Black type signifies important transfer O.W./N.W.

After *The Evolution of Man and Society*, C. D. Darlington. Allen and Unwin 1969.

change in one or more organs. This organic change may in its turn involve a modification of the bony framework which holds the soft parts in place. An increase in lung size which accompanies high altitude living is thus reflected in a bigger thorax, jutting ribs and a raised rib cage. In other words the need for oxygen is met by a barrel chest. The whole sequence of events in change goes from physiology to soft-part anatomy to the skeleton. And we see the gross effects of mountain living in the mountain zones from Western Europe to the Himalayas where the people are stocky and big-chested.

Perhaps early man was subjected to severe selective forces when he reached the Andes and the Himalayas. Here the oxygen-thin air might have weeded out the flat chests and left the barrel-chests to continue the population. But the *diversity* of the founder population in its capacity to adapt must have been all important for its success.

The severe cold of the last glacial phase in Siberia might have been the selective agent which carved out the flat, frost-adapted face of the extreme type of Mongoloid. The engineering of the face is based on the reduction of the area of exposure to frost. It is possible as Coon suggests that this type of face evolved in a population trapped by encircling glaciers. When the glaciers melted the populations of these highly specialized men expanded, perhaps 10,000 years ago, carrying their frost-adapted features to China, Japan, Tibet, S.E. Asia and Indonesia, giving to this day a strong Mongolian stamp to the whole of the Far East. Mongolians too filtered across an arctic zone into the Americas, probably about 15,000 years ago. Evidence suggests that they hunted mammoth and other large mammals in the S.W. of North America 13,000 years ago while glaciers still covered the north of what is now the United States.

The men who peopled the New World did not bring in with them the pigment mutations of the Negro and the other black races of the world. Indeed America had no black people until they were brought in as slaves in A.D. 1520. Black skin pigmentation is a shield against strong sunlight and even though in the Americas there are many hot regions, the range of skin colour varies from light to dark brown and no black-skinned peoples are found there. Indeed in Central America the aborigines have survived in tropical heat and sunshine for at least 10,000 years without black skins, but native people on the Gulf of Venezuela still paint their faces black to avoid sunburn. All this shows that the valuable mutations from brown to black skin colour appear to be rare in man. It might also show that glossy, yellowish or yellowish-brown

NHM—E

skins which are thick and reflect light, may be as efficient as black skins in preventing sunburn.

One last example, eye colour. The densely pigmented iris of the Negro, ranging from dark brown to black, stops an injurious amount of light (particularly ultra-violet) from damaging the interior of the eye. Lightly pigmented people can see the violet-blue end of the visual spectrum more accurately than darkly pigmented people can. Thus blue-eyed people may be able to distinguish distant objects more accurately than dark-eyed people, in dim, misty light. Such an adaptation as Coon suggests would have been one advantage to hunters in Western Europe during the Ice Age.

# 9: Two Evolutionary Cross Roads

UP to about 10,000 B.C. towards the end of the Ice Age and the end of his second great expansion, mankind had spread his wide-meshed net of sparse populations over most of the earth. Perhaps at this time there were some ten million people spread out over the earth in thousands of breeding groups or 'tribes'. A very few of these still survive today almost as they were then. We might use these *living* hunters and gatherers as a window to peer back on the past. Coon has explained that these present-day tribes are organized into breeding isolates averaging about 350 individuals, rarely reaching double that number (see Chapters 14 and 31). The numbers are kept down by the amount of food available. Encroachment on the territory of another group leads to danger and warfare. Social cohesion is reinforced by the need for protection against attack, the co-operation necessary for food gathering and hunting and the dependence upon the possession of tools. Living in isolation from each other, each tribe builds up its own culture: dialects, languages and religion, all of which reinforce the 'separateness' of tribes and interferes with cross-breeding (see Chapter

12). Today, cross-breeding has removed most of the differences, but as late as when Columbus reached America, about twenty million people in the New World were speaking some nine hundred languages with an average of 22,000 people per language.

These tribes had, and their survivors have two remarkable properties. As indicated they were all different from one another and appeared to be adapted genetically by physique, temperament and intelligence to their climates, habitats and ways of life. They were adapted to making their living by hunting, fishing, digging and collecting. Next, each tribe was uniform in its basic adaptation. Each individual was capable of doing all the jobs necessary to maintain life. There was none of the diversity of trades and professions found in a modern complex society. The only differences in the work individuals did depended upon sex and age. No class structure was known and leadership was feeble or nonexistent.* And what people could do (and still can) in the matter of maintaining life in adversity was often far beyond the capacity of civilized men and women (see Chapter 31).

The feebleness of leadership and class structure mentioned above is seen in the Congo Pygmies where one leader told an anthropologist that there was 'just no point in giving orders because no one would take any notice'. In Eskimos no rank and class exists. Each family is a cohesive, stronger group than the tribe as a whole and each is free to get on with its own affairs.

During this period of around 10,000 to 5000 B.C. the ice, after 100,000 years of relative stability (although in this time there had been peaks and lulls in the ice—peaks at 72,000 and 24,000 years ago) began to melt before the warmth of the interglacial period we now enjoy. As the ice melted, the water caused the sea to rise some 400 feet, and locally where the ice lay, the land, relieved of the weight of the ice, slowly rose up to 100 feet higher than it had been. America and Asia, Australia and New Guinea, Britain and Europe became separated by sea. The Alps became passable, the Mediterranean impassable. Thus the great streams of men bubbling out from the evolutionary cauldrons of Africa and Asia, were disturbed by cross-movements of men following the melting ice. In Europe, the warmth had caused dense forests to grow in the lowlands and the reindeer, following the cold, moved North in the wake of the retreating ice. The hungry neolithic men whose tools were too small to cope with the thick forests, moved to the coast or the edge of lagoons to eke out a new living eating shellfish, small game and fish. Besides

* See Darlington's essay in *Race & Modern Science*.

these cross-migrations of men there must have been sudden stoppages, when the men were faced by the sea.

A theory put forward by Darlington is that these migrations probably led to the mixings of previously isolated tribes. Novel gene combinations may have been brought together by cross-breeding, leading to a great diversity of people and this could have led to the origin of new peoples with new capacities. These new people according to Darlington were able to make the next revolutionary step forward by domesticating the cereals.

We know the general location of two such evolutionary cradles: the

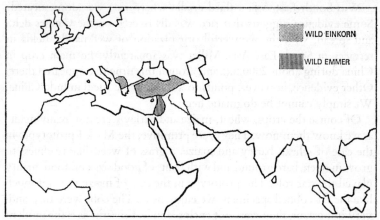

FIG. 12 The distribution of wild wheat. From *The Neolithic Revolution*, S. Cole. British Museum, Nature History, 1967. We know where the wild ancestors of our staple crops like wheat and maize grew because most of them are still growing there. In settlements like Jarmo in Kurdistan (see text) grains of the first cultivated wheats have been found hardly changed from the living wild wheats growing nearby. A few feet above the first cultivated wheats, and preserved in the soil above them (indicating a more recent origin), grains of the hybrid, high yielding bread wheat have been found. Likewise the modern, heavy maize has been bred from the wild teosinte grass which still grows in Mexico.

Near East in around 8000 B.C. (wheats), in an area which surrounds the basins of the Euphrates and the Tigris and lies between Palestine, Syria, Kurdistan and Luristan (see Fig. 12), and Central America in about 5000 B.C. (maize) in a region which runs from New Mexico to Guatemala and Ecuador. To be precise, the oldest known remains of maize come from the Coxatlan Cave in the Tehuacan valley, Mexico, dated by radiocarbon to about 5000 B.C., and carbonized grains and clay impressions of spikelets of a form of wheat were discovered in Iraq (at Jarmo) dating from about 6000 B.C. Why in these places? Probably because they represented two world cross-roads for the migrating peoples where genetic mixing and strong selective pressures bred the men who learned how to propagate crops to produce the first tribes of cultivators. Clearly physical conditions would have been important. Cereal agriculture needs defensible settlements; mountainous valleys with good outlook posts. Also conducive to cereal agriculture may be restricted land for this would limit hunting territory and would favour cultivation of plants and confinement of beasts.

Was South-East Asia a third cradle where rice was domesticated? Some evidence suggests that rice was discovered on the Ganges delta and spread, with the wonderful organization of wet paddy fields in terraces, *to* South-East Asia. Millet was apparently the main crop in China during about 2000 B.C. and around this time rice appeared there. Other evidence, however, points to a third cradle (rice) in Indo China. We simply cannot be dogmatic here.

Of course the crops, wheat, maize and barley were not 'ready made' as we know them now. They were primitive, the Mark I prototype: in the case of wheat, barley and maize, a grass of weed-like readiness to grow in open, bare ground and with fruits of good size and food quality played the star role. This prototype in the case of maize was not much like the fat-cobbed specimens we enjoy now. The cobs were tiny and, very important, they were not enclosed in leaf sheaths as is the modern cob. The latter depends on man for its propagation and man depends on the cob for food (see Chapter 10). These 'star' crops had others growing alongside. Indeed in Mexico, gourds, lima beans and squashes were probably cultivated before maize. In the Near East, peas, lentils and flaxes were part of the complex.

These two cradles, the Old and the New World, were sharply different and their peoples likewise. The variety of communications in the Near East centre, the choice of climate with mountains, rivers, deserts and seas in close proximity to it, may have been responsible for a greater diversity of peoples here compared with the Middle American centre. The peoples in the former therefore may have increased and diversified faster.

# 10: The Creation of Agriculture

**B**EFORE the dates mentioned above, men had only collected grain from wild annual grasses and stored it for eating. These wild food plants, the prototypes mentioned above, must have germinated raggedly over the season and ripened unevenly. Now man began to sow and till and harvest regularly. Unconsciously he selected the crop plants that grew close together in large quantities, whose seed ripened and germinated quickly and together so that it could be harvested collectively. And he had to recognize and use two other genetically determined traits in the wild grains related to wheat, barley, rice and other grains: the difference between shattering and stiff, non-shattering seed heads, controlled by one or two pairs of genes and between plants whose hulls stuck closely to the grain and those where the hulls allowed the grain to fall out early.

Shattering seed heads break up into pieces containing one or two seeds as soon as the seed is ripe. Under wild conditions this is useful to the plant to spread its seeds but it is disadvantageous to man because grain can only be harvested by hand. In modern strains of cultivated grain (wheat) the seed heads are stiff and hold their seeds until they are harvested by scythes or combines. Mutations that cause the grains to fall out of the hulls easily during threshing are likewise desirable. Wild grasses carrying mutations for non-shattering and 'loose hull' must have been long ago selected by man from among diverse populations of wild cereal species. But note, these qualities made the plant *dependent upon man* for its propagation.

Thus from the wild plants, these new plants changed out of all recognition to be like the maize and wheats we know now. Hereditary mutations, such as the ones described, led to new characters and also to an increase in the yield of grain. In the New World, in Central America, the cultivation of maize, beans, potatoes and cotton led to similar improvement of plant races, by largely unconscious selection. And in the Old World, in the well-watered grassy uplands that circled the Arabian, Syrian and Iranian deserts (the Near East) wheats and barleys came into being. Excavations at Jarmo in Iraq for instance showed that people here domesticated the goat, grew barley and two different kinds of wheat around 7000 B.C. It was perhaps only a village of three and a half acres with 150 people in it. Many other digs have revealed similar evidence in this region.

As the knowledge of cultivation improved, the 'farmers' supplied with a regular and increasing source of food, spread east and west from the Near East focus described above, and more slowly, north and south. These expanding populations were the 'Neolithic farmers'. Their way of life and methods of cultivation exist to this day in certain primitive tribes: the American Indians whose economy is essentially that of hunting and gathering supplemented by incipient agriculture, and certain other American Indian tribes (together amounting to 2·6 million), who live by food gathering and hunting or by practising shifting cultivation using hoes or digging sticks.

But back to the spreading populations. Westwards they spread from the Near East focus taking with them the first crops, wheats and barleys, into Central and Western Europe, up the Danube and across the Rhine, along the Mediterranean coasts into France and from there into the British Isles across the Channel. The local climates here were suited to the Near Eastern plants and domesticated animals, so there was no need to substitute local species. For this reason the spread of agriculture was fast across Europe taking only from about 6200 B.C. to 4500 B.C. to spread from the area of the Black Sea to the North Sea. The spread was slow to Britain where the farmers arrived about 3000 B.C. (see Fig. 13).

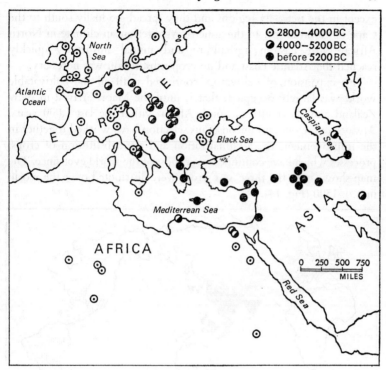

Fig. 13 Initial dates of Neolithic agriculture. From *The Living Races of Man* by C. Coon, Cape, 1967.

Eastwards they spread into Inner Asia, through India about 4000 B.C., reaching China and Indo China about 3000 B.C. In China it first appeared on the rich loess fields of the Yellow River. In many of these regions wheat did not grow so well and new plants had to be substituted. In the drier and poorer lands of Abyssinia, in India and N. China a number of different millets were used. Rice was probably not brought into China until about 2000 B.C. from either Indo China or from India as mentioned earlier. The plants from the Near East, particularly wheat, barley and flax, were not suited to the summer rains of the lands south of the Sahara desert. The local plants domesticated in the Sudan around 2000 B.C. were several varieties of millet, cowpeas, okra, water melons and sesame. And in the bend of the Niger, a variety of rice was domesticated.

The domestic animals had no trouble in the savannas and grasslands except in the tsetse-fly regions and they spread gradually south to the Cape of Good Hope. In the zone of Mediterranean climate in North Africa, Near Eastern agriculture and animal husbandry quickly reached the Atlantic coast and no crop substitution was necessary.

This expansion of cultivators continued until all the cultivable world was largely occupied; that is until the Maori arrived in New Zealand and the Bantu in South Africa within the last 1,000 years. Always, conscious and unconscious selection have worked together in the improvement, the acclimatization and the substitution of crops, processes which have continued over most of the world ever since. The map shows how the three 'star' crops were distributed over the world in A.D. 1500 (Fig. 14).

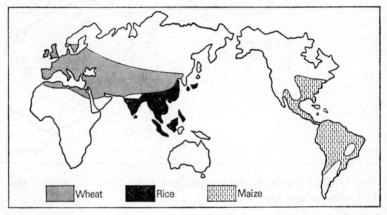

FIG. 14 The three great cereal areas of the world: the distribution of cultivated wheat, rice and maize in 1500 A.D. From *The Neolithic Revolution*, S. Cole, 1967.

The tribes of cultivators who were successful had the knowledge and skill to handle the seed, the plant and the soil. Prior to this stage man and crop went 'their own ways' and, by chance only, man cultivated the crop. Now man began to depend on the crop for his life and his future as the crop depended on him for its propagation, as described above for maize and man and wheat and man. This combination of 'man-and-crop,' as Darlington suggests, became a new closely integrated unit in evolution. And slowly in this way, after a hundred generations races of grain cultivators arose, selected for certain qualities of body and mind; patience, industry and foresight, a love of home, a feeling for the earth and crops, a strong sense of property and often cleanliness, qualities inherited by the successful grain growers of the old and the new Worlds today.

## ROOT CROPS AND MAN

Both in the Old and the New Worlds, the easier cultivation of the root crops attracted and fostered people of a less industrious kind than the alert grain growers. The propagation of roots can be picked up in the course of a lifetime by palaeolithic tribes in India now, and do not require the hundred generation apprenticeship or selection of the first grain growers. When picked up, the cultivation of roots, like those of yams in Africa, 'advances that part of the population that contributes least to the common good'.* Soil deterioration sets in. As emphasized in Chapter 4 the choice of environment may be an instinctive one but it is one that mostly suits the diverse heredities of man.

## ANIMALS

In the Old World the domestication of animals followed agriculture after perhaps 20 or 30 generations. Probably sedentary farmers domesticated cattle rather than hunters. But what motivated domestication of cattle and other animals? One theory suggests that motivation was religious because the horns of the wild cattle (and sheep and goats) resembled the moon's crescent and the economic use of the animals was a byproduct of a domestication, religious in origin. Perhaps the bison was never domesticated because it lacked crescent-shaped horns.

Already the wild ancestors of goats, sheep, cattle and pigs existed in the Middle and Near East (Figs. 15, 16, 17), in the area where wheat and barley were brought under cultivation. The dog must have been tamed very early, perhaps about 15,000 B.C. in northern Europe, from races of small wolves. The dog helped man to hunt and draw sledges as well as to clean up his camp by scavenging. It may have been exploited too, after some refinement, to herd wild goats and sheep. The 'man-dog' unit, therefore, made possible the earliest forms of domestication. Then came the sheep and goat from the highlands of Persia and Anatolia, domesticated around 6500 and 7000 B.C. respectively. Later from the lowlands of Mesopotamia, came the ox and the pig perhaps from the

* See Burkhill (bibliography)

**TABLE 4**

*Domesticated Mammals of the Old World*

| Paleolithic (O.W. & N.W.) | wild distribution | sites and dates of domestication | geographical expansion | main uses and aims of selection |
|---|---|---|---|---|
| 1. Dog | N. temp. many races (wolf) | many independent 15,000 B.C. (?) | universal including paleolithic. Australian (dingo) | 1. hunting 2. hauling 3. herding (in domestication of ruminants) 4. guarding 5. meat |
| 2. Reindeer | subarctic forest and tundra races (E) | N. Eurasia 10,000 B.C. (?) | panarctic | free ranging, migrating and breeding |
| *Neolithic (O.W.)* | | | | |
| 3. Goat (R) | C. Asia and S.E. Europe | Persia, Anatolia 7000 B.C. | followed both agricultural and pastoral expansions; often displaced by sheep | 1. meat 2. milk 3. skin and hair |
| 4. Sheep (R) | as above | Caspian steppes 6500 B.C. | main agent of pastoral expansion throughout O.W. | 1. meat 2. milk 3. wool |
| 5. Cattle (R) | Persia, S. Europe, India (E) | 1. Anatolia 6000 B.C. 2. Indus valley 2500 B.C. (independent) | agricultural and pastoral | 1. meat (except in India) 2. milk (except in China) 3. haulage, everywhere 4. thrashing corn |
| 6. Water Buffalo (R) | India (E) | Indus valley 2000 B.C. | to China and Europe with agriculture | as above |

| | Tibet to Mongolia (E) | Nepal c. 1000 B.C. | continued to arctic climate (over 2000 m.) | meat, milk, haulage and carriage |
|---|---|---|---|---|
| 7. Yak (R) | Tibet to Mongolia (E) | Nepal c. 1000 B.C. | continued to arctic climate (over 2000 m.) | meat, milk, haulage and carriage |
| 8. Pig | Europe to China (wild boar) | Anatolia 6000 B.C. China ? 2000 B.C. (independent) | originally woodland; later near universal with agriculture | meat and skin (and collecting truffles) |
| 9. Ass | N. African steppes | Egypt 4000 B.C. | with pastoralism (Babylonia 2000 B.C.) | 1. carriage 2. riding 3. milk |
| 10. Onager | S.W. Asian steppes | Sumeria 3000 B.C. | (E) displaced by horse 1500 B.C. | haulage |
| 11. Horse | Eurasian steppes tundra and forest | Caspian 2250 B.C. | with pastoralism to Egypt 1600 B.C. to China 1500 B.C. | 1. meat 2. haulage 3. riding especially in war 4. milk |
| 12. Camel (R) a. Dromedary (one-hump) | Arabia (E) | 1200 B.C. | N.W. Africa to India (southern) | 1. carriage 2. riding 3. milk |
| b. Bactrian (two-hump) | C. Asia | 500 B.C. | Anatolia to Mongolia (northern) | as above |
| 13. Elephant a. Indian | Syria, India, China | Indus: 2500 B.C. | S. Asia | 1. jungle haulage 2. battle |
| b. N. African | N. Africa (E) | Egypt: 280 B.C. | Italy: Hannibal | battle only (E) |

R: Ruminant.
E: Extinct as wild or as domesticated animals.
After *The Evolution of Man and Society*, C. D. Darlington, Allen & Unwin, 1969.

O.W.: Old World.
N.W.: New World.

forests of the Zagros and the Taurus mountains. The oldest pack animal was the ass from the Sudan, used in Egypt in 4000 B.C. The horse came later; domesticated in about 2250 B.C. in Central Asia it arrived there from its native North America over dry sea beds while the oceans were locked up in the ice caps. Other animals domesticated for transport purposes in the Old World were the camel (about 1200 B.C.) and the elephant, domesticated in Egypt about 280 B.C. and separately in the Indus in 2500 B.C. And in the New World the llama was brought in as a pack animal. For a summary of this information see Table 4.

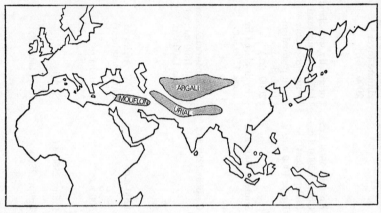

FIG. 15 Distribution of wild sheep, *Ovis*. From *The Neolithic Revolution*, S. Cole, British Museum, Natural History.

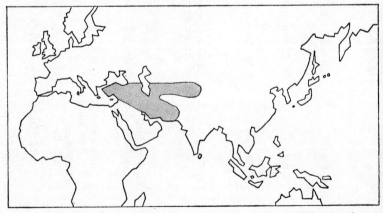

FIG. 16 Distribution of wild goat, *Capra*. From *The Neolithic Revolution*, S. Cole, 1967.

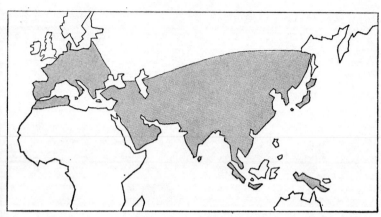

FIG. 17 Distribution of wild pig, *Sus scrofa*. From *The Neolithic Revolution*, S. Cole, 1967.

As with the crops, these animals may have been unconsciously selected for their usefulness to their keeper. And *vice versa*. Just as the grain growers were more intelligent and alert than the root growers, so the horse and cattle men were more enterprising than the swineherds. It appears to have been these adventurous horsemen who were responsible for the rapid spread of Neolithic peoples in the Old World.

# 11: The Origins of the Class System

THE origins of the class system as Darlington suggests did not stem directly from the meeting of the spreading tribes of farmers and hunters. They were on an equal footing. It might have originated from cross breeding between them because such 'outbreeding' (see Chapter 12) leads to genetic recombination and allows new arrangements of genes to be tried out in the hybrid offspring. The theory is that new groups of specialists, herdsmen, craftsmen, mariners, traders, warriors and priests originated by such hybridization and not by the *original* parent groups merely inbreeding. Such inbreeding would lead to stability of type: people who thought and behaved in a similar way to their parents. A few of the new *hybrid* groups would however, have novel gifts. These new groups would have been small at first, single families perhaps, but those that were successful multiplied and migrated. One of the groups of specialists was the metalworkers (who to this day form castes serving the communities they live in—the Asuras of Southern Bihar State are hereditary iron workers and castes of iron-working Negroes act as smiths in the Berber lands of Africa) and we can see how other castes could have expanded by considering them. The processes of metalworking, always enveloped in magic, the inventors kept secret and passed down the generations from father to son. The secrecy was strengthened by an economic motive. To keep the know-how in certain families the metalworkers' sons married into metalworking families; in other words, like married like. The incentive (and instincts) of assortative mating, or like marrying like, has continued to this day to maintain the myriads of groups, cliques and classes in our own complex society.

These gifted metalworking families spread to wherever they could find markets, provided by the herdsmen and cultivators. But although they settled among them, each group retained its individuality. That is, although they mingled together and traded, they seldom mated. Indeed they stuck to their own life and ways. Thus, like present society, the whole community (peasants, herdsmen, the metalworkers and cultivators) benefited through mutual co-operation but remained genetically separate. We may say that these simple communities became disrupted genetically and divided occupationally. And these groups or classes can be recognized today among the peasants and herdsmen of the Ancient East, India, Europe, Africa and newly colonized territories. All these groups or classes owe their distinctive character, as we have emphasized, to their different origins, different heredities and different capacities to make their own living by their own kind of work.

In modern nations like our own, the classes, like the tribes we have been speaking of, are maintained by assortative mating. But, of course, they are infinitely more complex. They are split by occupation, by recreations, by religions; they are split into groups or sects, into castes or classes, into cliques or gangs. They have different interests, aptitudes and abilities. And since they marry within groups, each has a different genetic outfit, a different heredity. Yet (and this is the strength of society) just as it was 10,000 years ago, they are groups which co-operate by one kind of man helping another kind of man. One biological principle then, connects the society of our own age with that of the Neolithic period; namely a combination without co-habitation, of different tribes, races or stocks. By this combination, as Darlington has graphically stated in relation to modern society, 'the separate tribes once freely spread like an extended pavement, are now piled up into the towering masses of our social classes',* classes which work, think and speak differently but co-operate by virtue of inherited qualities which they preserve by not inter-breeding a great deal.

* *Brit. J. Psychol.* 54 (1963).

The combinations may arise in several ways and the classes can be *maintained* in many ways. Combinations can arise by friendly co-operation such as we have described above as between the peasants, herdsmen and metalworkers. Such a peaceful co-operation of racially different people seems to have been one of the foundations of class differentiation wherever sailors, craftsmen, merchants and missionaries have wandered and settled. But the class system can arise by fierce conflict, by warriors imposing their rule on peaceful cultivators. This happened in ancient Egypt, mediaeval Europe, in China and Japan and in many parts of Africa at many times.

Some of these warrior groups probably arose by *disruptive selection*. This is the process by which new breeds, castes (like the metalworkers) or races, originate from inside old groups. In return for protection the peasant supplied the food and other services. But, by a wry twist of fate, the status of the farmer, who always supported the system, was lowered and indeed has repeatedly been lowered throughout history. Why? Perhaps the hundreds of generations of the Neolithic age bred in him a love of his land and a refusal to budge from it. His peasant's caution preferred this security to that of chancing his arm to fight for more land.

After about 4000 B.C. the control of the stratification of society passed into the hands of the governing classes who might have been warriors or priests. The highest rewards went to these helmsmen of society. They kept the peace, organized war, controlled the distribution of food and told the nation when to increase the population or decrease it. They invented the marriage laws which laid down the closeness of inbreeding allowed or the width of outbreeding tolerated (see Chapter 12).

Few advanced societies have remained static in their class structure for long. They have been changed repeatedly by migration, famine, conquest, revolution and disease. But those nations that have survived and evolved have always had a well-defined structure based on the instinctive principle of inter-fertile classes which work together without breeding together. A dominant civilization, in short, is held together by a royal family, a priesthood to see that the marriage rules maintain the purity of its breeding pattern, a warrior class, a merchant or banking class to make the money, usually Jews, and at the bottom the men with the picks, shovels and ploughs. This new and instinctive social invention is, as we have seen, no older than perhaps 10,000 years. Before this, as in primitive societies now, the differences in social function and work arose only because of sex and age differences. This genetic homogeneity made possible cohesion without specialization and maintained the close adaptation of the tribe to the habitat. But it also maintained (and still does) a backwardness and inflexibility that societies with a class structure avoid. And it is *selection* which has changed the simplicity of the tribal organization into the complexity of modern society. It has allowed the proliferation of different groups and classes. Every step in civilization, every discovery, like the working of iron or the storing of the hard grains, has removed the specific pressure of natural selection from the population enjoying the specific benefits resulting from that particular discovery. And so it has allowed the growth of a wonderful diversity of groups with specialized abilities. But selection has done this at the expense of the loss of equally wonderful *unspecialized* abilities as found in the primitive group. Table 5 on page 85 shows how the Australian aborigine knows his game and other animals and has an immense and detailed knowledge of food plants. Such knowledge allows his survival and is probably adaptive. But he finds counting difficult and regular manual work tedious. Civilized man has lost such natural knowledge of his environment but has, of course, gained in a multitude of other ways.

It takes all sorts to make a world, so it is said. We may agree; because, genetically *different* groups permit the building up of complex societies and cultures and the exploration of the earth's resources by a numerous and diverse population.

# 12: The Development of the Breeding System

WE may ask ourselves now how the human breeding system arose. Breeding systems may lie between two limits: the limits to outbreeding and the limits to inbreeding. Let us consider these in turn.

The limits to outbreeding, that is marriages or matings between unrelated people, are set by space, work, language or dialect, religion and economic or social status. All these barriers to marriage are environmental influences which set a zone of choice within which a mate is chosen (although we all know that this zone is often polevaulted over). Within this zone there is the genetic component, assortative mating*, which drives like to marry like. These environmental and genetic influences tend to split society up into groups.

Space, religion and dialect are strong barriers to outbreeding at the lower social levels. Economic and social incentives (the old school tie effect) act at the higher social levels. Four examples of these breeding barriers are described below.

An investigation in Northern Italy showed that a man used to find

* See *Biology and the Social Crisis*.

his mate at an average of 600 yards but when bicycles were invented this jumped to 1600 yards! The fact that religion is a barrier is well known (although this is weakening a little): Jew marries Jew (see Chapter 29) and on the whole Catholic Catholic and Quaker Quaker. Small breeding groups have arisen from economic or political motives: the merchant princes of Chios, Venice, Amsterdam and elsewhere. Dialect in primitive groups can form a strong barrier. Darlington has remarked that dialect marks off as closely as possible, a breeding group; a unit in which genetic exchange takes place by marriage and out of which it takes place but rarely. Dialect effectively isolates groups on the flat plains of Hungary or in the deep valleys of New Guinea. Some of these inbreeding groups can be shown to be genetically distinct. Galton, for example, showed that the Quakers have a high frequency of inherited colour blindness, a genetically determined quality which makes them slightly different from other groups. Inbreeding among the scavenging caste of Gujarat near Bombay, whose job it is to collect refuse and night soil, has led to differences in their blood group genes from other castes. Is it possible that the gene differences represent a protection against infection? Although people in our own complex society show no difference on the *surface* as between groups and classes, it is likely that groups and classes still carry collections of genes that make them slightly different from each other. The different classes may have begun a hundred or two generations ago by differing on the surface; but they end by differing more under the surface.

Inbreeding, that is marriage or mating between related people, is regulated in all human societies by self-imposed rules. Some of these are important genetically because the marriages are between blood relations. Others are designed to reduce friction among people in any way concerned with the marriage.

Unusual inbreeding, as between brother and sister, is taboo and has been decreed a crime at many times in history. Usually the closest form of inbreeding allowed is between first cousins or uncles and nieces. Why? Because first cousin marriages, for example in societies where close marriage is unusual, do produce a higher frequency of abnormal offspring or are less fertile than marriages between unrelated people. But groups who have inbred for generations suffer no decrease in fertility*, nor are there an unusually high proportion of defective offspring. They have become 'adapted' to inbreeding.

But what are the deeper biological reasons for outbreeding? The

* See *Biology and the Social Crisis*.

reasons are probably evolutionary. Originally man must have been like dogs or other animals in not being able to recognize his kindred with which he must have mated. But now man has adopted rules which discourage brother-sister mating and indeed all other matings within a wide range of kindred.

Darlington suggests that early sub-human stocks must either have been repelled instinctively from mating with their kith and kin or attracted to them. If attracted they would have been bound to form small, inbred groups, genetically similar. These brother/sister, father/daughter matings would continually split-up populations into groups of unequal size and differing character. Instead of the population being 'open' to the shuffling of genes by cross-marriage, it would gradually splinter and disrupt. It seems reasonable to suppose, therefore, that the human groups who survived must have been those with an instinctive, that is genetic, repulsion for incest. These alone would be variable and adaptable, capable of doing new things, meeting new environmental challenges and thinking in new ways. Indeed all living societies may well have inherited a basic aversion to incest though on top of this considerable social and cultural mechanism appears to be necessary to keep this frequency low.

We may argue further, that large homogeneous co-operative groups could only come into existence when the gift of recognition of one's kindred could be exploited to *avoid* matings with them. In other words the gift was used instinctively to develop a system of outbreeding. Can we learn anything about such a key step in man's evolution as the origins of outbreeding from comparative studies of living primates, a group of animals which includes lemurs, monkeys, baboons, chimpanzees, gorillas and man himself? Note we are discussing outbreeding and not the 'incest taboo' which is a fairly recent culturally controlled barrier; the evolution of outbreeding as indicated earlier must have developed at a much earlier stage in man's evolution. The answer to our basic question is probably 'no' as yet. Primate mating systems are very variable and knowledge of them is based on a few field reports of wild groups and certain pioneer studies on zoo animals. But in general inbreeding and not outbreeding is the rule in primates. There is a huge gap between even the most primitive human society with its complicated taboos about sex (age of partners, time, place of intercourse and so on) and the most advanced sub-human primate one. Yet it is possible to see the glimmerings of an evolution towards the human condition from the indiscriminate matings of certain New World monkeys to the formation of exclusive stable pair-bonds between specific animals as in the Anthropoid gibbon. The overthrowing of primate nature—when it happened and how, is a mystery. The emergence of man from his primate background, however, must represent some *suppression* of man's primate nature by the specifically human 'thinking cap', the cerebral cortex. The advantage reaped by the subordination of sexual drive may have been of selective benefit to the groups practising it. If such primate tendencies as indiscriminate sexuality, dominance and brute competition were substituted for *cooperation* and stability of the family group (which incestuous relationships would disrupt) then genetical evolution would favour the *cooperative* groups; they would have survival value for instance in such activities as searching for a sparse supply of food, and in defence and attack.

A restriction of outbreeding would have been valuable too. One act of cross-mating between tribes, classes or castes, can undo the work of a hundred generations of faithful breeding within the group. Cross-breeding smashes gene outfits that have made their possessors adapted to their way of life; hidden genes are exposed to selection and non-adaptive variation is pruned away. Mating barriers between animals and between plants have evolved to preserve their genetic integrity. Perhaps in animals and man the instinct for assortative mating arose to preserve valuable gene combinations.

On a genetic basis, therefore, nations which have survived are those that have permitted by their breeding rules, a limited amount of cross-breeding between inter-fertile groups. Inbreeding preserves the homogeneous, conventional, well-adapted mass. Outbreeding allows recombination of gene outfits previously kept separate. Sometimes as indicated the offspring of these 'wide' marriages are not very fertile. But balanced against this, small numbers of successful offspring result. To quote three exceptional men who were the product of wide class-crosses: William the Conqueror, Abraham Lincoln, Lenin, men who changed history.

Eventually the instinctive limiting of inbreeding and outbreeding were replaced by social and intellectual control and were codified into breeding rules or laws with which every nation is familiar. The influence of these rules penetrates to the heart of every family. They are effective in the making or breaking of nations and in the growth and decline of religions. The more eccentric the system of rules, the more marked are the consequences they tend to produce.

## THE CASTE SYSTEM

One concrete, modern example, the caste system of India, is instructive here. In India, dense populations, sharply differentiated in colour, were able to preserve a balance by making a religion out of co-operation between groups which were encouraged to keep a respectful distance apart and never interbreed without penalty.

The system was invented by priestly castes some 3,000 years ago, who thereby gained a favoured position. It has gone on longer with less change than elsewhere. But the system is resilient for it is still capable of assimilating and preserving unlimited racial diversity. Even though the system is resilient, the marriage rules are made of iron. Recently such age-old institutions as untouchability, hereditary occupation and food pollution have shown signs of weakening but not the marriage laws. Three of these are important biologically.

The first, the most important attribute of caste, is that a person shall marry within the group of birth. The second is the rule of 'marrying out'. This prohibits marriages between individuals who belong to the same section of a caste. One of the most important practical consequences of this regulation is to limit the degree of inbreeding; for example by banning marriages between the children of two brothers. The third is the regulation of close marriage which differs in Northern and Southern India (see Fig. 18). This rule prohibits marriages between two individuals related through a common ancestor up to the seventh generation on the father's side and the fifth generation on the mother's side.

With this breeding system any lapse in the rule of caste is punished by the most stringent measures. With Hinduism, the only way to legally sow a few wild oats and plant a different gene outfit in another caste is by social demotion or outcasting. Social promotion, characteristic of European systems, is open only to women. The whole system can only be maintained by religious conviction and according to Darlington 'it shows its effect in reducing the flexibility and initiative of the peoples concerned and of their culture'.

Much work on the genetics of castes needs to be done. The little that has, revealed genetic variation (in blood group systems, red-green colour vision defect and ability to taste a certain chemical*)and this may be largely due to adaptation of castes to their local environments over a span of many generations. Take two of six castes investigated

* phenylthiourea

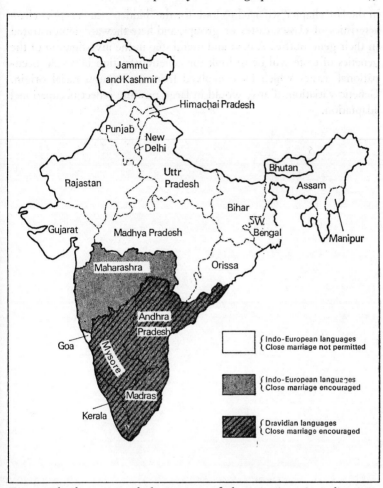

FIG. 18 The language and the patterns of close marriages in India. From 'Genetic Adaptation in Man' by L. D. Sanguvi in *The Biology of Human Adaptability* (ed. Baker and Weiner), Clarendon Press, 1966.

in the state of Gujarat, farmers and scavengers. The farmers are significantly different, in the genes controlling certain blood groups systems and in the genes controlling red-green colour blindness, from all the other castes investigated. The scavengers have the lowest incidence of genes for colour blindness, the higher incidence of the B-type blood gene and the lowest for the O gene of all the castes. As was mentioned in the last chapter we need to look for the 'hidden', the 'cryptic' characteristics of classes, castes or groups, and here they are demonstrated in their gene-outfits. A next and useful step in the investigation of the genetics of caste will be to look for genetic variation between 'occupational' castes which have evolved from a common racial origin. Genetic variation, if any, would in large measure reflect occupational adaptation.

# 13: Cities in the Making

AN offspring of the agricultural revolution was the city. By domesticating food plants, man reduced the space required for sustaining each individual by a factor of 500 at least. Indeed it has been suggested, from the evidence of present-day primitive tribes, that even when man had developed tools and weapons for hunting he probably needed four square miles of land to pick over for each person in his family (see Chapter 15). But now man could live more closely.

Cities grew up at the beginning of the Bronze Age around 2000 to 4000 B.C. First in the valleys of the Tigris and Euphrates, Nile, Indus and Hwang Ho (see Fig. 19).

Why in these places? Mainly because they were all rich alluvial valleys. The Nile meant life. It overran its banks and left refreshed, fertile earth as it receded; bumper crops could be raised with primitive equipment and in the papyrus swamps of Upper Egypt there was a rich supply of water fowl and game and dangerous hippopotami. The Indus Valley, although marsh, fever and jungle ridden, was likewise very fertile. Each year the soil was renewed by annual flooding and the river itself was full of fish. Farming prospered; wheat and six-rowed barley were grown, field peas, melons, dates. Later across Arabia

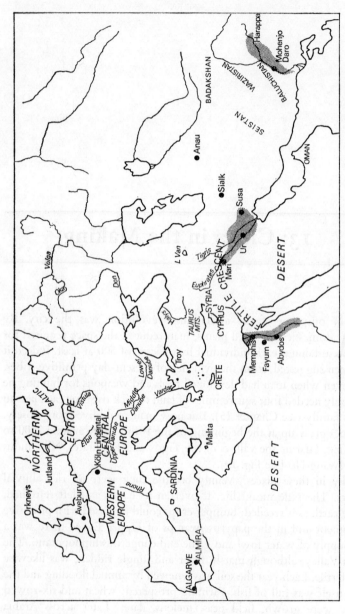

Fig. 19 Areas of civilization about 2500 B.C. From *What Happened in History*, Gordon Childe, Pelican.

perhaps, during the third millenium, the first two African crops were brought in: cotton and sesame. The communities here in the Indus valley kept their animals: dogs, cats, fowls, humped cattle, buffaloes and probably pigs and horses. And the first area for city development on the Tigris-Euphrates delta, the ancient Sumer, an area no larger than Denmark, was likewise rich (see Fig. 19). This raised silt platform was covered in vast swamps and towering reeds. Muddy waters snaked slowly to the sea. But the waters were full of fish, the reeds teemed with wild fowl, wild pig and other game and the soil was prolific. Documents dating from 2500 B.C. recorded an average yield of barley, as 86 times the sowing. The farmers then in this Garden of Eden could produce a food surplus.

The abundance of food meant that people could live closer together and in large groups. The 'hard' grains, in particular, could be stored year after year and stave off a lean year. All this meant larger, more durable villages with markets where people could exchange goods. To this day, primitive hunters, fishers and gatherers pitch their settlements close to one another for trading but although they meet they do not freely mingle.

Abundant food alone would not have been a sufficiently powerful catalyst for the creation of cities. The vital key to their success seems to have been genetic diversity. In these rich valleys people congregated who had diverse skills, temperaments and instincts, but who were, nonetheless, able to co-operate with each other without disruption of the community. Probably a few of these men were leaders—a complex social hierachy like a growing city needs strong political control. Such control is known to have existed through royal families in Egypt or through priestly castes as in Sumer. Even one individual vested with authority and endowed with gifts of character and personality can increase the efficiency of 100 men five to ten hundredfold.

The firm leadership coalesced diverse people in the Sumerian cities in about 4000 B.C. At any rate in about 3000 B.C. the built-up area of Ur occupied 150 acres, perhaps holding a population of 24,000 souls. And the populations of three other cities in Sumer, Lagask, Umma and Khafajah are reliably estimated to have been 19,000, 16,000 and 12,000 respectively during 3000 to 2000 B.C. The story of the early Egyptian cities is lost in Nile silt under modern towns, but cities like Memphis at the apex of the Nile delta grew up around 3000 B.C. By 2500 B.C. populous cities had emerged in India too and these, like the Egyptian and Chinese cities like Lo-Yang on the Yellow River, owed their character to ideas carried from Sumer. The brick-built cities of Mohenjo-daro in the Indus Valley and Harappa (Fig. 19) 400 miles further north were very large. The ruins of the former cover at least a square mile and the walled area of the latter in 1853, had a perimeter of 2½ miles.

We may notice in the development of cities an autocatalytic effect. Population growth provided the spur for an increased pace of technical development; controlling water by storage, ditching, flooding, draining to increase food supply and this in turn accelerated progress in engineering, mathematics and physics.

## DISEASE, CROWDS, FERTILITY

In addition to genetic diversity and strong leadership three qualities were necessary for the growth of cities. First, the ability of people to tolerate disease in dense populations. Second, the frame of mind to stand crowds and live cheek by jowl with very unlike people; a matter of temperament. Third, the ability to maintain a population under these conditions which were quite *new* in history, for man as we know, was moulded by genetic evolution for low density living. Let us examine these three qualities in a little more detail.

First, disease (see Table 3). Measles, mumps, chicken pox, scarlet fever, smallpox, whooping cough, diphtheria and many other infectious diseases probably evolved relatively recently, 200 generations ago when cities started to grow. Here, conditions probably existed where bacteria and viruses could flourish near to man: walled cities, narrow streets, crowds in bazaars, filth in the streets as in Cairo or Calcutta today. In such conditions, virus and bacterial diseases would mutate and evolve to become more parasitic than ever before. These diseases are, moreover climatically indifferent because they are directly infectious and contagious. How different were these crowded city conditions from the open-air camp with its small, less cramped population.

City life then may have selected strains of men who were probably resistant to certain diseases to which primitive rural people often had no resistance. What kind of man might selection have produced? Coon suggests one with greater efficiency of the circulatory system, under conditions of privation, than men who lived a more open-air life. Perhaps, too, men with greater resistance to infection of the liver and kidneys. Both these qualities prove to be better in small, slender people than in tall, burly ones. Then, it would be of survival value if these men 'grew up' more quickly than their country cousins since this would shorten the period when infection might strike and kill or damage. Resistance to infection, we know, is least during childhood and old age, but only in the former will it be of selective value in evolution for group survival. Perhaps, then, over many generations, selection went hard against 'the slowly maturing, lanky, poorly co-ordinated adolescents so commonly seen in our antiseptic society'. Such lanky weeds were eliminated during the critical period of childhood especially if they were badly fed and reared in slum conditions.

There is another theory however. The small-sized city people might have been the result of selective migration from the country to the town. These shorter, thinner, lighter, narrow-faced people, often with delicate hands, perhaps migrated to the cities to find work to suit their capacities, leaving the big, heavy men on the farms.

Of course what has been said applies to the ancient cities of India, China and Egypt. Most city dwellers in the West today are only a few generations from the country. We are, we might say, 'primitives' who have escaped the disease selection of the East by accident.

Disease resistance and tolerance of a poor diet were not the only selective hoops the new city dwellers had to jump through to survive. They also had to face continuous, intergroup contacts. Here again, migration to the cities might have been selective, the city drawing to it a certain kind of person, one who could put up with crowds and live cheek by jowl with very different people.

The ability to live in close proximity with very different people to one's own, however, has never been fully acquired in any society. In Chapter 11 we noted that this inability to meet this requirement in a full sense is the reason why social classes keep apart. In cities too (although this is changing in most of the Western cities) people following the same trade live together. At first they must have lived in their own villages which became 'quarters' or certain streets. They kept apart and bred apart and son followed father in his trade or profession. This division of labour and the inborn instinct to keep separate are still part and parcel of old city life, in the East especially. Specialization must have arisen early so that a householder would go to one shop for meat, to another for honey, a third for bread, a fourth for candles, and so on. And the ancient foundations still to some extent remain.

It is obvious that the selective advantages of high fertility will be strong in dense populations, living under unhygienic conditions where disease is rife and there is a high rate of infant mortality. Cholera and plague do not choose between rich and poor, strong and weak. If only a fraction of the children born can hope to survive into the next generation, small families are likely to be wiped out completely.

Thus, in these disease ridden cities, in the past and now, selection for lines of high fertility must have been at a premium—more so than in the hunting and pastoral societies from which city people originated and where man had lived for more than ninety-nine per cent of his history. In these pastoral societies famine, not disease, might well have been the brake to population growth, for in these societies population was widely spaced and people were living in hygienic conditions. High fertility would be a disadvantage. In a poor year for example, an Eskimo (taking him as a present day example of a member of a primitive hunting society) might only be able to find enough food to keep one or two children from starving. Such a quantity of food would be useless shared between ten. All would starve. Carr Saunders claims that all observations emphasize the small size of the family of primitive people. It seems as if low fertility might have evolved in response to appropriate conditions of life. High fertility seems to be a *new* phenomenon characteristic of the last few thousand years and selected for in the specialized conditions of urban life.

# 14: Population Increase and its Control

THE domestication of animals and plants and improvements in the cultivation of crops in the Neolithic age obviously favoured an increase in population, because people could get a regular supply of food. Likewise, the invention of a social hierarchy, as in the development of cities, in which each man knew his job and with the whole community co-operating to a common end, tended to make life easier and increase numbers. In short, both more settled farming and the growth of cities led to some increases in population, not rapid, but still unprecedented.

But we are over-running our story. What regulated population size at the palaeolithic stage *before* the agricultural revolution in the Neo-lithic age some 10,000 years ago? The evidence as to what might have happened comes from three sources: observations on animal populations; records of travellers and missionaries on the habits of simple societies and, lastly, more recent observations of primitive peoples such as the Australian aborigines, who represent a latter day survival of man at a palaeolithic level of economy.

In all animal species the capacity for reproduction allows the population to increase quickly when the supply of food increases, until it reaches a steady density, at which balance exists and a proper 'social space' can exist between individuals. If the population over-runs food supply, it restricts its numbers by reducing or postponing egg production, by cannibalism, by killing off young and in some cases by violence. An example of violence can be seen sometimes in apes and monkeys when shortage of food, or sudden overpopulation impinges upon a colony and lethal struggles break out. Southwick has described experiments made at the Calcutta Zoo where 17 rhesus monkeys were kept in a cage area of 1,000 square feet and their aggressive behaviour (threat, submission, attack, fighting) was scored. One experiment divided the cage in two except for a door and this had little effect on aggressive behaviour. When the door was closed and the monkeys had only half the area (500 square feet) the frequency of aggressive behaviour was doubled. It was also significantly increased when food was provided in one basket probably because the monkeys had to come close together to feed. It should be emphasized, however, that this kind of violence has *not* been observed in the wild. Many observers on the watch for violence in, for example, gibbons, howler monkeys, African red-tail monkeys, Japanese monkeys have found it to be rare or non-existent.

In all cases investigated *experimentally* the death-rate in mammals and birds appears to be dependent upon population density and to cease below a certain critical point. Many of these regulating devices are continually in action without any threat of starvation. And these mechanisms appear to have evolved by selection to achieve drastic reduction of a population that is in danger of outstripping the resources. In times of over-crowding these regulating devices cause storks to throw most of the nestlings out of their nest and monkeys to change from protective behaviour towards females and young to an attitude of indifference, neglect and murder. In general, when crowding indicates that food supply is short, birds and mammals neglect, desert or kill the young (see Chapter 31).

What happens in primitive man? It was argued in the previous chapter that natural fertility among primitive people is not great. Darwin in *The Descent of Man* noted this when he wrote 'that the reproductive power is actually less in barbarous, than in civilized races . . . it appears that their families are usually small and large ones rare'. Another piece of evidence supporting the inherited lack of fertility in primitive, nomadic people is that they do not easily recover their numbers after being hit by disease brought in from outside. But apart from some natural infertility, the families of primitive people (such as Eskimos and American Indians) are *kept* small by infanticide,* which is always selective, usually against the female (the key agent of population growth) by abortion, by restriction of intercourse and human sacrifice of widows or captives. How did these practices evolve?

Carr Saunders writes, 'Those groups practising the most advantageous customs will have an advantage in the constant struggle between adjacent groups over those that practice less advantageous customs. Few customs can be more advantageous than those which limit the number of a group to the desirable number . . . there would grow up the idea that it was the right thing to bring up a certain limited number of children and the limitation of the family would be enforced by convention.'

As in the case of animals, the most primitive tribes may restrict family size by an automatic adjustment of breeding behaviour. And the behaviour would be geared to the needs of the moment. The shortcomings of too many mouths to feed with limited resources would be common sense. If, on the other hand, disease or severe weather caused a high death rate among infants, abortion and infanticide would be curtailed.

Recent observations on the Australian aborigines help here too for these people act as a window to the past, perhaps letting us see how people lived in the palaeolithic age before the domestication of animals and plants. The average size of an Aborigine tribe is about 500 people and the area they occupy, in the case of about 130 of the 400 tribes appears to be related to the mean annual rainfall within the tribal territory (see Fig. 20). Of course, rain means life and food. The larger the area, the lower the total rainfall and *vice versa*. The aborigines exploit the whole environment eating much which the Europeans would not see and much that would revolt him (see Table 5). Like animals then, the density of these human tribes seems to be subject to 'environmental determinism'—in this case rainfall. In other present-day people living at a primitive level of economy, other controlling factors might operate: the density of Eskimos might be related to the length of the growing season, temperature and day-length.

All this evidence shows that the density of palaeolithic man before the advent of agriculture may have been regulated by instinctive cultural practices favoured by selection.

* See *Biology and the Social Crisis*.

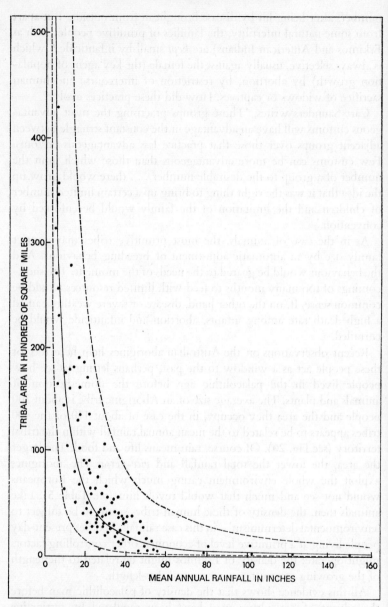

FIG. 20 Correlation between rainfall and size of tribal area. From an article by J. B. Birdsell in *Human Ecology* (ed. Bresler), 1967.

## TABLE 5

| Animal Foods | Plant Foods |
|---|---|
| (1) 6 sorts of kangaroos. | (1) 29 kinds of roots. |
| (2) 5 marsupials somewhat smaller than rabbits. | (2) 4 kinds of fruit. |
| (3) 2 species of opossums. | (3) 2 species of cycad nuts. |
| (4) 9 species of marsupial rats and mice. | (4) 2 other types of nuts. |
| (5) Dingoes. | (5) Seeds of several species of leguminous plants. |
| (6) 1 type of whale. | (6) 2 kinds of mesembryanthemum. |
| (7) 2 species of seals. | (7) 7 types of fungus. |
| (8) Birds of every kind including emus and wild turkeys. | (8) 4 sorts of gum. |
| (9) 3 types of turtles. | (9) 2 kinds of manna. |
| (10) 11 kinds of frogs. | (10) Flowers of several species of Banksia. |
| (11) 7 types of iguanas and lizards. | |
| (12) 8 sorts of snakes. | |
| (13) Eggs of every species of bird and lizard. | |
| (14) 29 kinds of fish. | |
| (15) All saltwater shellfish except oysters. | |
| (16) 4 kinds of freshwater shellfish. | |
| (17) 4 kinds of grubs. | |

From an article by J. B. Birdsell in *Human Ecology*, (ed) Bresler.

During the long millennia of the Neolithic age, however, two evolutionary changes were brought about which affected population. First, as we have already indicated, there may have been a decrease in the feeling for regulating family size and conserving territory as happens now, for example, in the Australian aborigines. These losses were no doubt due to the decay of the selective pressures supporting the genetically determined instincts. Second there may have been a *general* increase in the natural fertility of man. Slowly the brakes were taken off and very slowly population build-up began.

Much later than the Neolithic age, population growth found support and guidance from the great religions which have always been propagated by breeding. As Darlington has written, 'Their lasting success has been proportional to the care and discernment with which they organized the survival and sexual reproduction of the faithful.' The founders of Hinduism (see Chapter 12) and Judaism were explicit about these matters in both general covenants and specific laws. The founders of Christianity too, soon learned to direct their rules and rituals towards increasing the Christian population. In a recent Catholic Encyclical (*Populorum Progressio*) it is stated for example, that governments may encourage family limitation if population grows faster than 'available national income'.

The success of Islam in these matters may be quoted, for its expansion several times repeated, was the result of a well-balanced breeding policy and was an outstanding biological success. First, there was the forbidding of abortion, infanticide, and war to the death. Second, grand devices of multiplication were fostered: conquest, slavery, and the policy of one man having several wives (polygamy). Third and very important, medically sound rules for cleanliness were introduced.

The upshot is that, up to the time of Malthus, advanced societies multiplied, enhanced by the great religions and unchecked by instinct as in former times, or by reason. The most important factors determining population size may be summed up in three words: disease, famine, war.

Prior to the eighteenth or nineteenth century the pattern of population growth was not steady and smooth but consisted of a succession of periods of increase or decrease, between which lay periods of no change in local and in national population. And there was no *consistent* trend in world population over long periods of time. Growth or decline in one part of the world, often bore no relation to what was happening in another. For instance in 1346 the Plague was raging in China and from there it reached Europe in 1348 to kill perhaps one in two or one in four (evidence is slim) but it may not have been so drastic in the Far East. It was as well that the high death-rate was matched by a high birth-rate and to most people this was as natural as the rising of the sun and as uncontrollable.

Sustained population growth at the rate of one per cent per year or more, which began in the British Isles and Scandinavia in the late eighteenth century began in China with the establishment of peace under the Manchu Empire in the seventeenth century, in India with the establishment of the British Empire, in Latin America not until the nineteenth century and in Africa not until the present century.

# 15: Destruction of Habitat and Migration of Peoples

WITH the build up in population, habitat, partly under instinctive control before the development of agriculture, has been continually destroyed.* Palaeolithic man took care to adjust his numbers by birth control, abortion and infanticide and not to slaughter the pregnant animals or eat the seed on which his descendants would rely for their food.

To encounter the effects of 'over-kill', Palaeolithic man in his evolution developed the lore of totem and taboo and cropping and rationing rules. This wisdom, Fisher writes, learned by our ancestors, has largely been forgotten. The rot set in during Neolithic times and accelerated after A.D. 1600, the later years of post-Renaissance explorations and the early years of the Industrial Revolution.

Neolithic man and his successors, instead of being tenants on earth became the worst kind of landlords, often taking what they could get and giving little or nothing in return to repair or replenish. This parasitic existence is nowhere better seen than in the early development of cities. In 1500 B.C. the brick-built city of Mohenjo-daro in the

* See *Biology and the Social Crisis*.

Indus valley was already dying. Why? Firing of vegetation, felling of timber to bake the clay bricks—the use of clay for millions of bricks, age after age, had bared the earth. Abnormal flooding too had salted the land and turned the soil sour. The landscape was utterly worn out.

Ancient Rome too, worked ruin in the surrounding landscape. Long before it reached a million inhabitants the city had over-reached itself in terms of food, water, fuel and building materials. Moreover its internal birth-rate had become inadequate to replace, let alone strengthen, its population. To facilitate the movement of its legions and speed up administration, roads were carved recklessly through the landscape with no thought about the nature of the terrain. And the same happened with the construction of reservoirs and aqueducts which were vital to the water supply. Trees were felled continually to feed the growing technology and to provide fuel for central, hot-air heating. The sewers, instead of returning the precious minerals found in night-soil to the land, poisoned the Tiber. At this stage the balance tipped from harmony with the landscape to parasitism.

## TREE FELLING

Tree-felling to make cities, to build ships, for use as fuel and to clear ground for farming, proceeded on a vast scale in all centres of population. Egypt during the Third Dynasty, almost 5,000 years ago, used the forests of the Eastern Mediterranean for wood to supplement stone in the building of its cities. The timbers were carried in wooden ships as well, some of them 170 feet long. Legend records that Solomon, for the construction of his temple and palace had 'four score thousand hewers in the mountains' to cut down cedars from the hills of Lebanon. The Phoenicians as early as 2000 B.C. were using the cedars of Lebanon to sell them to the almost timberless land of Egypt for the building of this temple. Today these hills are bare. The making of Carthage and Alexandria tell a similar tale and indeed so do all the huge modern cities.

Huge wooden ships have already been referred to and the construction of these must have demanded vast quantities of timber.

The Phoenicians in 2000 B.C. were using the cedars of Lebanon to build up their huge mercantile empire which had the whole of the Atlantic as its preserve. And the Minoans around 1500 B.C. ruled the Mediterranean by cutting down the forests of Crete to build their fleets. In addition they exported timber to Egypt and indeed oil from the olive which was planted to replace the forests. This merciless lopping of timber had grave effects. Darlington, writing of Crete, notes that, 'The deep green landscape turned first grey and then white; the soil accumulated in a million years was being washed from its hillsides in a few centuries.'* It would be too simple a notion to suggest that the collapse of the Minoan civilization was simply due to the wrecking of the habitat by tree-felling alone. In any case this is only a theory. Others have been put forward: defeat by Mycenaean Greeks and an enormous volcanic eruption in about 1470 B.C. on the island of Thera some 70 miles north of Crete. The destruction theory is based on the belief that parts of Crete were destroyed by the rain of ash and huge tidal waves—a mile high at the vortex and rushing outwards at 200 miles per hour. Destruction of Crete whether by the ruin of its soil by felling or by volcanic disaster led to a migration of minds that were to influence the future of Western civilization.

During the Roman period, the volume of grain carried by Mediterranean shipping traffic was unrivalled until modern times. Millions of bushels of grain were carried to Rome from Egypt and North Africa. Some of the ships were large by modern construction standards and carried up to 1,200 tons of grain. They maintained a substantial and continuing demand for timber.

The consequences of this widespread tree-felling were diverse. Hot and dry countries were parched and destroyed. Hilly countries like Crete had the soil washed from the hillsides. Wet and cold countries like Britain were ruined by lack of drainage. What had been forest was put under the plough and in Ireland the ploughed land, no longer drained, became bog in perhaps 2000 B.C. And where the soil was sandy, forest clearance by fire and axe led to heath formation—which has remained since Neolithic times at such places as Thetford Chase in Norfolk, and the heaths of Jutland in Europe.

In Mesopotamia forest clearance to provide grazing land, started soil erosion and the rot of the irrigation system which gradually silted up. Huge quantities of silt were washed down from the denuded uplands and vast labour forces had to be employed to keep the irrigation channels clear. When the ditches were finally wrecked by the Mongol invaders in the thirteenth century B.C., the piles of silt by the ditches showed that the system was choked up long before it was destroyed.

These few examples show the grim effect of increasing population

* *The Evolution of Man and Society.*

on the habitat, in the ancient world. The axe, the plough, the olive and the nibbling sheep and goat destroyed much of the soil of countries like Syria, Palestine, Greece, Italy and North Africa.

## THE BRAIN DRAIN

The destruction of habitat led to the migration of peoples. Many migrations have taken place in human history for many reasons as Part 5 shows. Most of them have been *selective* in that they have modified the intelligence of the community. On a small scale we may note that the most enterprising, active and intelligent farmers move on to the best land. They exercise discrimination and choose their environment. This is why in all countries, the standard of farming varies from district to district. And on a larger scale, as each society in turn destroyed its habitat, it lost its population. It was always the governors, the administrators, the priests and craftsmen who went to where the living was better. Carr Saunders notes that migrating races show 'enterprise, hopefulness and courage'*; in other words the loss was selective. We see it today in the brain-drain. We may note its effects in the city and the country and between country and country. The brain-drain on the countryside exaggerates the contrast between the slow, bucolic peasant and the alert and progressive citizen and if the brain-drain goes on from Britain with continued genetical impoverishment, our descendants may live at a lower standard than we do. We must remember, however, that emigration of talent may in the long run be balanced by equally able immigrants (see Chapter 25).

About the migration of people from Crete, Darlington writes, 'As the olive took the place of the cypress on the white mountains of Crete, modest farmers gathered their harvests. But the princes had departed. The princes sailed to new lands taking with them fortunately the vine, the olive and the alphabet, less fortunately the sheep and the goat.'† The results of Minoan migrations were quickly noticeable in Greece in about 1400 B.C. The refugees introduced the Greeks to their alphabet, art, archery and games—all apparently until then unknown on the mainland. They taught the primitive tribes to work in gold and bronze and may have assisted them to design the tombs and palaces that were the glory of Mycenaean culture.

* *The Population Problem.*
† see *Race and Modern Science.*

The Egyptians were the one people who failed to ruin their foundations. Their irrigation system has never needed to be seriously altered. Although Egypt has sunk in stature over its five or six thousand years of continuous cultivation and although its governing classes have risen and fallen, the cultivation and the cultivators have survived almost unchanged.

We may note in conclusion that soil and society are inter-linked. As the soil decays so does society. The great civilizations of Sumeria, the Indus, Crete, Carthage and Rome and many others declined and many vanished. It is true that besides the parasitism of man on his life blood, the soil, there must have been other influences at work—such as disease—which affected the decline, but destruction of habitat must have been a major cause. The lesson is that each technical advance leads to greater productivity and hence greater pressures on the environment and finally to disaster. The greater the technical advance the greater the disaster. It is only at the disaster point that conservation evolves by compulsion. Now technique advances exponentially so that it is imperative to prevent disaster by putting conservation methods into action *simultaneously* with every technical advance.

# Part 4: The Changing Patterns of Disease

# 16: Disease and Ecology

IT is useful to look at disease as an ecological phenomenon linked with many variables and having a profound effect on human population numbers in both time and space. These variables are numerous, ranging from inborn resistance (p. 47) sex (Fig. 28) and stage in the life cycle of man (p. 131) to various environmental factors such as food supply and type of food, type of clothing (p. 107), domestic equipment and housing, geographical area (Fig. 21), social class (Fig. 22) density of population, movements of disease-carrying animals, including man himself (p. 113) and weather (p. 115). And, as in most ecological problems, the single cause concept is suspect. Rather, different checks and balances cause one factor to act more forcibly than another at different times and places. Food shortage or excess of food may be the 'master factor' producing disease at one time or place, at another the fact that clothes are not easily washed, at another that plague-carrying rats have been driven by flooding to higher land and at another that ten people have to sleep in one small room.

The idea that some of the diseases of modern life—measles, mumps, chicken-pox, diphtheria—may have evolved in the last five or six thousand years, when denser populations started to form with the growth of cities and more settled agriculture, was put forward in Chapter 13. Before this, as we have seen, man existed in small groups. Such host populations as these and the relatively short time between then and now would not allow the evolution of *brand new* parasites. Where might they have come from? Probably the microbes causing some of these 'modern' infections were derived from already existing strains in evolutionary older species of animals—monkeys for example. The crowds and filth of city life might well have provided fertile ground for these viruses and bacteria to evolve and adapt to man. Smallpox may have evolved from a cattle virus. The virus of measles may have infected a different host before the growth of cities. As the virus is like that of distemper in dogs and rinderpest in cattle it is quite likely that man caught the disease from one of these sources when he domesticated animals. That virulent strains did arise is clear, for often disease wiped out all but a privileged minority. These lucky few probably had the genetic outfit to resist the disease and were thus able to propagate their own kind. They may, of course, have been cleaner and better fed.

## GENETIC SYSTEMS OF MICROBES AND MAN

Such genetic diversity in the human population is important for its survival because the microbes in their turn, would ring the changes genetically, evolving new strains of their own. The general point is that both man and microbe possess genetic systems which adapt each population to an *average* condition of life. But each genetical system makes sure that if the majority is snuffed out by disease or some environmental change, appropriate minorities exist to carry on life. Perhaps the rise and decline in human mortality in the richer countries in the past (and in poor ones now) was the effect of an alteration in the balance between the virulence of the infective organisms and man's differing resistance to them. The decline in mortality from scarlet fever, for example, in the last quarter of the nineteenth century probably represented a reduction in the virulence of the bacterium by mutation; in 1848–72 it perhaps caused one death in 25 but in 1947 less than one death in 10,000. The influenza virus rings the changes too. It has a habit of changing its protein coat from time to time and each time it does so the human population on which it feeds and reproduces is faced with a new unknown marauder of which the chemical defence systems of the body has no experience. The defences of the body will not recognize the influenza virus because the pattern of its coat has changed. Therefore, unlike measles and chicken-pox, the immunity conferred by one attack of influenza does not leave sufferers immune to another. Once someone has recovered from measles the chance of this type of virus mounting a second successful attack on the same person is slender because the body recognizes the pattern of the coat and will produce an overwhelming amount of appropriate antibody chemicals to destroy the virus. The increasing resistance of the body caused by better food, clean water and fresh air, too, has helped to diminish such diseases as tuberculosis.

Our ancestors in the past thousand years in Britain and Western Europe have had to cope with savage killers like the influenza virus just mentioned, which is said to have caused the deaths of 21 million people in 1918. Plague, leprosy and the sweating sickness; great pox, small pox; diphtheria, cholera and tuberculosis all hacked down our numbers in the long past and indeed many of them do so now.

Those of us who read this page are the descendants of those privileged minorities who were spared the ravages of disease by resisting them and surviving to leave offspring. In the England of 1550, for example, so heavy was infant mortality that on *average* the expectation of life worked out at eight and a half and in Geneva in the same year it was four years nine months.* By the eighteenth century the great killing diseases had reached their peak. The infectious diseases of infancy, including the dreaded infantile diarrhoea and the three captains of death, tuberculosis, syphilis, and malaria combined with the pandemic diseases of cholera, plague and typhus to make life brief and uncertain. Cholera, for example, was a public menace in the U.S.A. as late as 1893, and from 1832 until that date killed hundreds of thousands of Americans. Surprising as it may seem, the *average* expectation of life from birth never exceeded 19* years in Britain until about 150 years ago. One wonders how man escaped extinction. But epidemics, like forest fires, burn out in the end, when the survivors have thinned out and become immune to the illness.

In 1969 disease patterns have changed for some of us. Here and in the U.S.A., for example, we no longer live under the shadow of the eighteenth and nineteenth century killing diseases, but have the twentieth century ones instead. Two out of three of us will die in bed of

---

* See contributions by Banks to the symposium *Man's Role in Changing the Face of the Earth* (Chicago) and *Health of Mankind* edited by G. Wolstenholme (C.I.B.A.). The ages above include infant deaths in the calculation.

one of the trio; heart attack, stroke or cancer at the age of 65 to 75 years old. And of the other third a large number will die in accidents. Many of our contemporaries in Latin America, Africa and Asia, on the other hand, are still dying of diseases that our great grandfathers were suffering from in the mid-nineteenth century. Their lives are as short as those of our ancestors (on average 50 years) and end too early for the degenerative diseases to set in and kill. A few figures will underline this point. In 1968 some 10 million people out of around 60 million died from malaria and tuberculosis in the 'developing' countries and the trio mentioned above accounted for about the same number, most of them living in the richer countries. Nearly half of the total deaths in the world are of newborn babies, infants and toddlers in Asia, Africa and Latin America. These underprivileged children, whose resistance is undermined by malnutrition, fall prey to infectious diseases such as tuberculosis, diphtheria, typhoid and virulent measles, or die from 'tropical diseases'.

This, briefly, is the changing pattern of physical disease. Medical and social advance has beaten the illnesses caused by external agents but not those of internal origin. And when these are beaten in the twenty-first century the next layer of the onion will show itself. As life is prolonged by new and better drugs and prolonged surgery, infectious diseases may (as they do now) reappear in the niches created by sheer age. For example, increased longevity in people suffering from diseases like cancer creates another fraction of the population highly susceptible to infection. And the battlefront between man and bacteria kept, in a sort of truce by physical fitness, will flare up into a struggle which in the end will certainly be won by the bacteria.

# 17: Barometers of
# Socio-Medical Progress

IN 1866 Florence Nightingale was asked to open a new children's hospital in Manchester. In her brief and blunt way she wrote and turned down the invitation. She thought that, 'Building more children's hospitals is not the proper remedy for infantile mortality and sickness—the true remedy lies in improving the children's homes.'

Infant mortality (death-rate in the first, often murderous, first year of life, per 1,000 live births) maternal mortality (death-rate of the mother per 1,000 total births), expectation of life and death-rates (mean annual number of deaths per 1,000 living) are together a sensitive indicator to the state of physical health of a community. We shall not here go into what may be the barometers of mental health. Sufficient to say that the incidence of violence, crime, alcoholism, delinquency and inadequacy are probably good indices.

High infant and maternal mortality and low expectation of life in particular, reflect degraded environments: insanitary conditions, overcrowding and malnutrition, a triumvirate that breeds disease. Florence Nightingale was right in her priorities; to build a hospital amid slums was to put the cart before the horse. On a world scale, a drop in the rates of the four indicators of health named above has been achieved by the keeping of peace and by social and medical advance. These have to some extent counter-balanced the three scourges of man: war and other violence, famine and, especially in the richer countries of the world, epidemics. Most of the progress is probably the result of *social* and, in the last generation, medical advance. By social advance is meant such matters as providing adequate quantities of safe drinking water, the removal of human excreta from continuous human contact, and the breaking up of overcrowded slums, or in a phrase, improvement in simple cleanliness. Table 6 gives some indirect evidence of progress in the health of Glasgow schoolchildren from 1910 to 1960.

## TABLE 6

*Health of Glasgow Schoolchildren, 1910-60*

(1)

| Period | Cleanliness | | Clothing | | Footgear | |
|---|---|---|---|---|---|---|
| | Verminous | | Insuffi-cient | Ragged and Dirty | Unsatis-factory | None |
| | Heads | Bodies | | | | |
| 1910–19 | 20·3 | 2·8 | 1·3 | 5·9 | 2·3 | 5·2 |
| 1930–39 | 6·7 | 0·2 | 0·1 | 0·5 | 0·4 | 0·0 |
| 1958–60 | 7·7 | 0·0 | 0·0 | 0·1 | 0·1 | 0·0 |

Percentages.

(2)

*Heights and Weights*

| Period | Boys | | | | Girls | | | |
|---|---|---|---|---|---|---|---|---|
| | 5 years | | 13 years | | 5 years | | 13 years | |
| | Ht. | Wt. | Ht. | Wt. | Ht. | Wt. | Ht. | Wt. |
| 1910–19 | 40·4 | 38·5 | 55·2 | 74·5 | 39·7 | 37·7 | 55·5 | 76·8 |
| 1930–39 | 41·3 | 39·7 | 56·8 | 81·6 | 41·0 | 38·3 | 57·7 | 85·9 |
| 1958–60 | 42·6 | 42·4 | 59·7 | 95·0 | 42·3 | 41·0 | 60·0 | 100·0 |

Inches and lbs.

From *The Uses of Epidemiology* by J. N. Morris, Livingstone, 1969.

Social advance plus medical progress has given us longer life. But why is it that a starving Asiatic today has a higher expectation of life (over 50) than a well-off, well-fed, well-looked-after landowner of a county family in the England of 1700 (average life expectation 37)? Mainly because of *medical* progress. Entire populations can be vaccinated even though they are at a primitive stage of agriculture; D.D.T. can by sprayed over a whole area wiping out malaria. In Ceylon, since D.D.T. got rid of the malarial mosquito, the death-rate fell from 22 to 12 per 1,000 in the seven years from 1945 to 1952. All the medical know-how of the West which took generations to accumulate, is available to the poor countries at one stroke. Take India. The improvement in public health in the sub-continent since independence has increased the average expectation of life from 32 to 50 years. As a result of the campaign to eradicate or control malaria, smallpox and other mass killers, the death-rate has dropped from 27 to 17 per 1,000 and infant mortality from 183 to 109 in 1968.

## THE UNEQUAL CHANCE OF DEATH

Table 7 clocks the progress made in saving infants' lives between about 1800 and 1965. In Britain for example even in 1900 infant mortality was 150 per 1,000. In 1938 it had dropped to 55 and in 1965 it stood at 19. This is the mark of social progress in providing cleaner food and drinking water, in more effective disposal of excreta, in better ventilation and more fresh air, and also the advance of medicine in the development of antibiotics since 1939. While the records show slow progress in Britain with hardly any improvement in infant mortality figures between 1800 and 1900 and then a more rapid fall, they show a rapid descent in places like Ceylon and Chile because the medical know-how is available at once, without the slow build up towards it. But no amount of medicine will improve on a dirty water supply and fly-covered excreta. Averages can be misleading too. The map (Fig. 21) shows how unequal the chances were of a baby living to be over one year old in different parts of England and Wales in 1954–8. If we probe deeper we shall find that the death-rate for infants will be higher in the houses of manual workers like miners than in the homes of say clerks (see Fig. 22). The same is true for middle-aged men and women: within England and Wales there is a steady increase in death-rates from the Southern and Eastern counties to the industrial conurbations

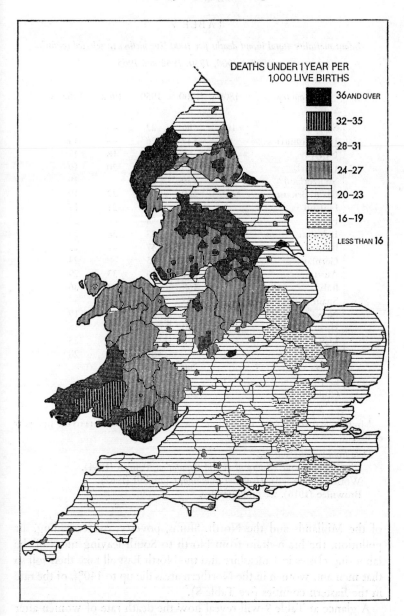

FIG. 21 Infant mortality. From *National Atlas of Disease Mortality in the U.K.* (ed. M. Howe), Royal Geographic Society, 1958.

## TABLE 7

*Infant mortality (total infant deaths per 1000 live births) in selected countries*
*c 1800, c 1900, 1950, 1962 and 1965*

| Country | 1800 | 1900 | 1950 | 1962 | 1965 |
|---|---|---|---|---|---|
| Sweden | 190 | 96 | 22 | — | 12 |
| Low Countries | | 147 | 26 | — | 14 |
| Norway | | 88 | 27 | 18 | 17 |
| Denmark | | 126 | 32 | 20 | 19 |
| Switzerland | | 139 | 32 | — | 19 |
| Great Britain | *155 | 150 | 33 | 22 | 19 |
| Finland | | 135 | 42 | 21 | 17 |
| France | 190 | 149 | 53 | — | 22 |
| Belgium | | 153 | 53 | 28 | 24 |
| Ireland | | 102 | 47 | — | 25 |
| Germany | | 207 | 55 | — | 24 |
| Austria | | 221 | 66 | 33 | 29 |
| Italy | | 168 | 68 | 42 | 36 |
| Spain | | 195 | 69 | — | 37 |
| New Zealand | | 75 | 23 | — | 19 |
| Japan | | 160 | 60 | 26 | 18 |
| U.S.A. | | 162 | 33 | 25 | 25 |
| U.S.S.R. | | — | 81 | — | 28 |
| India | | 200 | 137 | — | — |
| Ceylon | | — | 75 | 53 | — |
| Chile | | 264 | 153 | 121 | — |

* In first two years of life in London. The rest of the data refers to the first year
of life.

*Data from various sources.*
     Cipolla, *Economic History of World Population*, Pelican (1964).
     Wolstenholme (ed), *Health of Mankind*, Churchill (1967).
     Brownlee (1916), see bibliography.

of the Midlands and the North. Slums, poverty, overcrowding, air
pollution, the brain-drain from North to South leaving more of the
labouring classes in Lancashire and the North East all take their toll so
that men and women in the Northern areas die up to 140% of the rate
in the Eastern counties (see Table 8).

A glance at Table 9 will reveal how the death rate of women after
childbirth has dropped in England and Wales during the last century.
The reasons appear to be mainly due to cleanliness and ventilation in

## TABLE 8

### Death rates in middle and later life

| Conurbations | Age 45–64 M. | F. |
|---|---|---|
| Mersey | 17 | 8 |
| S.E. Lancs | 17 | 8 |
| Tyne | 17 | 8 |
| West Yorks | 16 | 8 |
| West Midlands | 15 | 7 |
| London | 13 | 7 |
| England and Wales | 14 | 7 |
| Eastern counties | 12 | 6 |

From Logan, R. F. L., Health Hazards, *Middle Age*, B.B.C. publication (1967)

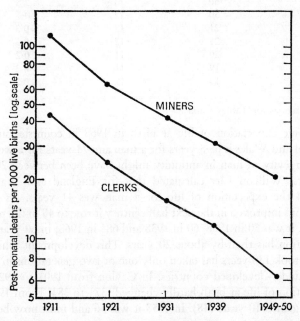

FIG. 22 Mortality at four weeks to one year of age in the children of miners and clerks. England and Wales. *Lancet*, 1955, I, 554.

the labour ward. In the mid-nineteenth century hospital death-rates were many times higher than those among home deliveries. The reason in most cases was infection during the period immediately after child-birth.

TABLE 9*

*A century of change in the health barometers of England and Wales*

| Period | Infant mortality per 1,000 live births | Crude death rate per 1,000 live population | Maternal mortality per 1,000 total births |
|--------|------------|------------|------------|
| 1867      | 155 | 22 | 6·0 |
| 1871–1880 | 149 | 21 | — |
| 1881–1890 | 142 | 19 | — |
| 1891–1900 | 153 | 18 | — |
| 1901–1910 | 128 | 15 | — |
| 1911–1920 | 100 | 14 | 4·0 |
| 1921–1930 | 72  | 12 | 4·0 |
| 1931      | 66  | 12 | 4·1 |
| 1941      | 60  | 13 | 2·8 |
| 1951      | 30  | 12 | 0·7 |
| 1961      | 21  | 12 | 0·3 |
| 1963      | 21  | 12 | 0·3 |
| 1964      | 20  | 11 | 0·2 |
| 1965      | 19  | 11 | 0·2 |
| 1966      | 19  | 12 | 0·2 |

* Sources as for Tables 7 and 8.

Average expectation of life at birth in 1968 in countries such as England and Wales is 68·5 years for a man and 74 years for a woman. The longevity of man in antiquity might have been between 20 and 30 years. William Farr calculated that for England and Wales in 1838–54 the expectation of life for a man was 41 years. As social conditions improved in the next half century it rose to 49 in the period 1901–2. It was 50 in 1908, 60 in 1938 and 68½ in 1968; in 60 years, life expectation has risen by about 20 years. This development which in Britain took 130 years has taken only one or two generations in some of the under-developed countries. In Ceylon from 1901 to 1921 the expectation of life at birth hardly changed: 37⅓ to 38⅓. From 1921 to 1946 it gained 10 years (48). In 1953 it was 56 and must now be well over 60.

Table 10 compares in space and time the 'standard of living' with duration of life. As our unit of comparison, the average standard of living of Western Europe on the eve of the 1939 war, is taken to equal 100. The 'standard of living' index equals the quantity of products consumed per inhabitant. As the standard of living rose in Europe from 1788 to 1938 so the expectation of life doubled from 30 to 60. But even with a standard of living half that of France before the Revolution, the people of Asia and Africa have a much longer duration of life which was not, in fact, reached in Europe until about 1870 with a standard of living about four times as high. Clearly the key factor here is not so much economic improvement as advances in socio-medicine. The *average* expectation of life has to be correctly interpreted. The rise has been caused chiefly by a decrease in *infant* mortality.

TABLE 10

*Standard of Living*

|  | Standard of living | Duration of life | |
| --- | --- | --- | --- |
|  |  | *in years* | *in indices* |
| France 1788 | 25 | 30 years | 50 |
| Western Europe in 1870 | 40 | 40 years | 66 |
| Western Europe in 1938 | 100 | 60 years | 100 |
| Present-day Asia | 10 | 40 to 45 years | 66 to 75 |
| Present-day Africa | 12 | 40 years | 66 |
| Present-day Latin America | 35 | 50 to 55 years | 84 to 92 |

From *Fertility and Survival*, A. Sauvy, Chatto and Windus, 1967.

Death-rates depend not only on health but also on the composition of the population by age groups. Even in the healthiest condition, a population of people over 70, say in an old people's home, would have a higher death-rate than that of a boys' school even if the latter existed in Dickensian squalor. Countries like England and Wales and the U.S.A. have, therefore, higher death-rates than under-developed countries, because the former have more old people than the latter. Fig. 23, which shows the age compositions of Britain and Ceylon in 1955–6 reveals the relative youth of the population of Ceylon compared with that of Britain. And the death-rates of the two countries underline the point: 9·8 for Ceylon in 1960, 11·7 for Britain. Like the

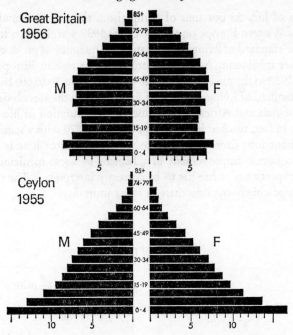

FIG. 23 Age composition of an old settled country (Britain) and an 'Old' Asiatic Country (Ceylon). From *Man and his Environment*, B.B.C., 1964.

drop in infant mortality and the rise in life expectation, death-rates have changed over a very short time in developing countries (see Table 11). In Ceylon in 1940 it was 21 per 1,000; in 1960 it was 9.0. In England in 1701–10 it stood at 31, a century later 23. Now it is 11. Most of the progress has come in the last 60 years and the fruits of that progress are quickly available to less developed countries like Ceylon, with striking results.

Here are two examples to back up our thesis that it is socio-medical, rather than economic progress that has caused the fall in the death-rate. Sauvy tells us that in France during the occupation in World War II, living conditions were difficult in terms of food, but the maintenance of order, and in particular such necessary medical aids as the isolation of infectious diseases and vaccination, kept the death-rate at about 17, which is below the rate for the peaceful years of 1911–13 when the death-rate was 19. In the U.S.S.R. in 1938 the death-rate was 18 per 1,000. Since then it has fallen to about 8 in 1960. But according to Sauvy the standard of living in terms of quality of food and housing

## TABLE 11

*Death rates per 1,000 in selected countries 1700–1965*

| Country | 1700 | 1750 | 1800 | 1850 | 1905 | 1950 | 1960 | 1965 |
|---|---|---|---|---|---|---|---|---|
| England & Wales | 31 | 31 | 23 | 23 | 15 | 12 | 12 | 11 |
| Finland | | 29 | 25 | 29 | 18 | 10 | — | 10 |
| France | | | 26 | 24 | 19 | 13 | 12 | 11 (west) |
| Germany | | | 27 | 27 | 18 | 10 | — | 11 |
| Low Countries | | | 26 | | 15 | 7 | — | 8 |
| Norway | | 25 | 24 | 17 | 14 | 9 | — | 9 |
| Sweden | | 27 | 23 | 22 | 15 | 10 | — | 10 |
| Switzerland | | | | 23 | 16 | 10 | — | 9 |
| U.S.S.R. | | | | 40 | 29 | 10 | 8 | 7 |
| U.S.A. | | | | | 15 | 10 | — | 9 |
| Chile | | | | | 32 | 15 | 12 | — |
| Japan | | | | | 21 | 11 | 8 | 7 |
| India | | | | | 43 | 16 | — | — |
| Egypt | | | | | 26 | 19 | — | — |

Data from Cipolla, *The Economic History of World Population*, Pelican (1964).
McKeown & Record (1958), see bibliography.
Wolstenholme (ed), *Health of Mankind*, Churchill (1967).

has not improved much. Animal foods, especially meat and butter were, in the 1950s, in short supply in Russia, while the average amount of living accommodation in the cities was 8¼ square yards per person, half the allowance of French Council Blocks. In spite of these spartan conditions the death-rate has fallen and expectation of life has risen more than ten years.

Table 9 summarizes the drop over a century in the death-rate, infant mortality and maternal mortality in England and Wales.

We may conclude this section by saying that up to about 1900 for developed countries like our own, the improvement in health was largely due to improving social conditions; clothing (in particular the change from woollen to boilable cotton clothes), food (and the type of utensil the food was cooked and eaten in) and housing; in general an improvement in simple cleanliness. This conclusion still holds good for the period 1900 to 1939 and in some areas of health Britain still has far to go, as Tables 7 and 11 show. But the causes become less easy to define because of the extension of the public health service and slum clearance programmes. After 1939 great changes have come because of the many discoveries in the methods of prevention and treatment of disease. Immunization and the use of antibiotics in particular have made the old epidemics of the past insignificant to us. Of more significance to us now than the *microbiological* diseases like typhoid and cholera are those diseases that must be caused by *tracechemicals* of which pesticides in food and carcinogens in smoke are outstanding examples. The picture, although improving, is different from that for Latin America, Africa and Asia. Here diseases caused by dirty water and daily contact with excreta loom large. Here only one quarter of urban populations are connected with sewers, another quarter use outside privies; a half have nothing. As far as water is concerned, the woman carrier of water is the rule; in fact two-thirds of the urban populations carry water, only one third have piped water. Although medical advance in these countries is used to great effect as we have seen, in some ways it is like spraying scent on a dung heap. The foundations to health in many cases are rotten and depend not only on medicine but on politics.

# 18: Some Examples of Changing Disease Patterns

## A WARNING NOTE

## A WARNING NOTE

GOING right back to A.D. 664, when plague was first described by Bede, until the present it is not easy to pin down
accurately, in many cases, what diseases are being described.
Records are often meagre. Diseases and causes of death are described as
'plague' and 'pestilence' which might have been many different
things. 'Sweating sickness', 'griping in the guts', 'strange fevers' and
'fluxes' all appear as causes of death. Griping in the guts for example
took an enormous death toll of infants in London in the hot summer
of 1669 when, according to Creighton, 4,385 infants died. This
disease, 'convulsions' and 'bowel-hive' were what we now call infantile
diarrhoea. It would be wrong to assert however, that no accurate des-
criptions of disease were given. In the latter part of the seventeenth
century the doctors Willis, Sydenham and Morton described accurately
the epidemics of their own time and this distinguished beginning continued right through the eighteenth and nineteenth centuries.

Prior to 1837 *national* birth- and death-rates were not recorded. After
1837 birth- and death-rates are in no doubt. Although cause of death

has been officially recorded since 1837, difficulties still arise in discussing trends, because of vagueness and inaccuracy of diagnosis and the changes in the names of diseases. There was a confusion between scarlet fever and diphtheria until 1855 and typhus was lumped with typhoid until 1869. Then there was uncertainty about a diagnosis such as tuberculosis, in an age when an X-ray of the chest was unknown and the infective microbe could not be identified until 1882. Even the method used to separate infectious from non-infectious diseases as causes of death raises problems; death said to be caused by diseases of the heart and nervous system probably included a large number resulting from undiagnosed infectious diseases such as rheumatic fever, syphilis and meningitis. Even today with plenty of doctors in richer countries the vagaries of diagnosis make it difficult to compare deathrates from certain diseases. English doctors tend to attribute the death of a case of chronic bronchitis to bronchitis while elsewhere death has been ascribed to associated diseases such as heart diseases and infections. This disparity makes any international comparison of bronchitis deaths difficult to interpret.

## EPIDEMIC 'SICKNESS' IN BRITAIN

We got a little bothered in December 1968 about a type of virulent 'flu that might have spread to us from Hong Kong. In the event it proved to be of little importance. Even if it had spread it would have been as naught compared with the ravages of the epidemics of the past. Creighton tells us that from A.D. 664 to 1666 the predominant infection was the bacillus-spread plague, although under its banner rode other cohorts of deadly disease which crushed hundreds of thousands: the sweating sickness of 1485–1551; the French pox (syphilis) of 1497 and subsequent years; 'small pokkes and mezils' of the early sixteenth century and for good measure the last great plague attack of 1665-6. Interspersed with these epidemics were 'pestilences' linked with famine. After the last plague vanished, its place was taken by a 'numerous brood of fevers' not easy to identify in modern terms. These fevers stretched out through the seventeenth to the late nineteenth centuries. Then smallpox, rare before the Stuart period, soared into prominence in the mid-seventeenth century rising in frequency through the eighteenth century to dwindle in the nineteenth. Epidemics of measles and whooping cough carted off their loads of death as did infantile diarrhoea. Except for infants and those over 45 mortality began to decline after 1850. After 1900 the big improvements in health began.

## A FEW EXAMPLES OF 'OLD' EPIDEMICS

The cycles of plagues in England have been described in another book.* But that of A.D. 664 is worth mentioning, because it is the first one recorded here and connects one end of a rising and plunging population graph which laconically marks the death by plague of hundreds of thousands of our ancestors, with the final plague of 1665-6. The plague of 664 broke out suddenly and after 'depopulating' southern England 'seized upon the province of Northumbria, where it raged for a long time far and wide, destroying an immense multitude of people'. It entered Ireland in August of 664 and 665 and is said to have killed two thirds of the population. This fact cannot be established but old documents do tell us that a long list of notables died in the pestilence.

Besides pestilence, the history of epidemics in England before the Black Death of 1349 is mainly a history of starvation with attendant sickness. We read in the Anglo-Saxon chronicle of 'very hard winter; pestilence and murrain' in 1046, of 'great mortality of men and cattle' in 1048, 1049 and 'most dire famine in all England; pestilence and murrain' in 1125. There are countless other stark records like these quoted in Creighton up to 1322. Merry England it might have been but it was notorious abroad for its famines of which those of 1193-7, 1257-69 and 1315-16 were the worst, exposing the disgraceful gap between rich and poor. A narrative of 1196 from the pen of William of Newburgh describes 'famine-pestilence' in Yorkshire. 'After the crowds of poor had been dying on all sides of want, a most savage plague ensued, as if from air corrupted by dead bodies of the poor. This pestilence showed but little respect even for those who had abundance of food; and as to those who were in want, it put an end to their long agony of hunger.'

## THE BLACK DEATH

The Black Death of 1349 killed about one in three of the English population, concentrated perhaps on adult males; whether monks and
* *Biology and the Social Crisis.*

friars died more frequently than peasants or whether all classes of society were attacked is an open question.

Three forms of plague were interwoven in the Black Death, bubonic plague carried by fleas and rats, pneumonic plague communicated from person to person by droplets and septicaemic plague which was the most lethal of all. Bubonic plague is excruciatingly painful. Huge boils, the size of an orange form in the groin and armpit together with high

TABLE 12

*Bill of Mortality of the Plague-year 1665 in London*

| Week ending | Christ- ened | Buried | Plague | Week ending | Christ- ened | Buried | Plague |
|---|---|---|---|---|---|---|---|
| Dec. 27 | 229 | 291 | 1 | June 27 | 199 | 684 | 267 |
| Jan.  3 | 239 | 349 | 0 | July  4 | 207 | 1,006 | 470 |
| 10 | 235 | 394 | 0 | 11 | 197 | 1,268 | 725 |
| 17 | 223 | 415 | 0 | 18 | 194 | 1,761 | 1,089 |
| 24 | 237 | 474 | 0 | 25 | 193 | 2,785 | 1,843 |
| 31 | 216 | 409 | 0 | Aug.  1 | 215 | 3,014 | 2,010 |
| Feb.  7 | 221 | 393 | 0 | 8 | 178 | 4,030 | 2,817 |
| 14 | 224 | 462 | 1 | 15 | 166 | 5,319 | 3,880 |
| 21 | 232 | 393 | 0 | 22 | 171 | 5,568 | 4,237 |
| 28 | 233 | 396 | 0 | 29 | 169 | 7,496 | 6,102 |
| Mar.  7 | 236 | 441 | 0 | Sept.  5 | 167 | 8,252 | 6,988 |
| 14 | 236 | 433 | 0 | 12 | 168 | 7,690 | 6,544 |
| 21 | 221 | 363 | 0 | 19 | 176 | 8,297 | 7,165 |
| 28 | 238 | 353 | 0 | 26 | 146 | 6,460 | 5,533 |
| Apr.  4 | 242 | 344 | 0 | Oct.  3 | 142 | 5,720 | 4,929 |
| 11 | 245 | 382 | 0 | 10 | 141 | 5,068 | 4,327 |
| 18 | 287 | 344 | 0 | 17 | 147 | 3,219 | 2,665 |
| 25 | 229 | 398 | 2 | 24 | 104 | 1,806 | 1,421 |
| May  2 | 237 | 388 | 0 | 31 | 104 | 1,388 | 1,031 |
| 9 | 211 | 347 | 9 | Nov.  7 | 95 | 1,787 | 1,414 |
| 16 | 227 | 353 | 3 | 14 | 113 | 1,359 | 1,050 |
| 23 | 231 | 385 | 14 | 21 | 108 | 905 | 652 |
| 30 | 229 | 400 | 17 | 28 | 112 | 544 | 333 |
| June  6 | 234 | 405 | 43 | Dec.  5 | 123 | 428 | 210 |
| 13 | 206 | 558 | 112 | 12 | 133 | 442 | 243 |
| 20 | 204 | 615 | 168 | 19 | 147 | 525 | 281 |
| | | | | | 9,967 | 97,306 | 68,596 |

From *A History of Epidemics in Britain*, C. Creighton, Cambridge, 1894.

fever. When they discharge they are evil smelling and the victim dies in miserable indignity shunned through fear and repulsion by his fellow men. Medical ignorance in Europe was almost complete beyond the notion that the plague was carried by a foul wind or miasma. No one suspected the rat or the flea and so the carriers roamed unhindered. The best poetic description of the plague is by the Welsh poet Ieuan Gethin (1349) 'We see death coming into our midst like black smoke, a plague which cuts off the young, a rootless phantom which has no mercy for fair countenance. Woe is me of the shilling in the arm-pit; it is seething, terrible, wherever it may come, a head that gives pain and causes a loud cry, a burden carried under the arms, a painful angry knob, a white lump. It is of the form of an apple, like the head of an onion, a small boil that spares no one. Great is its seething, like a burning cinder . . .'

After the Great Plague of 1665–6 (see Table 12) it waned, probably due to a change in the virulence of the microbe and not to traditional explanations such as an increase in food supply.

## ENGLISH SWEATS

The Tudor period was punctuated by at least five epidemics of a deadly disease called the 'English Sweats'—'a new kind of disease, from which no former age had suffered, as all agree.' A disease in which one could be 'merry at dinner and dead at supper'. In the light of modern knowledge it was probably a virus disease, perhaps a form of influenza spread by droplet infection. It appeared on Creighton's evidence in London in 1485, a fortnight after the arrival of Henry VII, fresh from his victory over Richard III at Bosworth Field. The symptoms graphically described by Dr Forrestier were, a sudden onset with 'grete swetying and stykyng, with rednesse of the face and of all the body, and a contynual thirst, with a grete hete and hedache because of the fumes and venoms'. In 1517 during the third epidemic, Cardinal Wolsey suffered four severe attacks and his life was despaired of and in the fourth outbreak (1528) Anne Boleyn had a mild attack. Henry VIII himself sped out of London (which 'wore the face of a dead city') trying to escape the disease. During this epidemic the disease spread to the continent, laying low the Germans but sparing the French. This gives us a clue to the origin of the disease. Perhaps the virus was carried to England by French mercenaries brought in by Henry Tudor in 1485.

The Seine valley from where the mercenaries came is a place with records of an infectious disease resembling the Sweats. Some of the French soldiers may have been carriers of the virus responsible in France for these mild endemic infections.* Most of the others must have been immune. When Henry VII's troops reached London the virus attacked the upper classes severely and because of this the disease was called 'stop-gallant'. The poorer people (who also suffered) were not so badly affected. Probably the poor, exposed to filth and crowds had developed immunity from past infections with weakly active strains of the same virus. But apparently the rich, who had never built up immunity, presented the virus with virgin soil.

## SMALLPOX

The gradual rise of smallpox to prominence in England about the end of the Elizabethan period and in the first years of the Stuarts is a striking example of how a disease can change in its choice of person to attack. It started off as a sporadic disease with its most serious effect on young adults, especially in the London epidemics of 1674 and 1681. In 1674 there were 2,507 smallpox deaths out of a total of 21,201; in 1681 2,982 deaths out of 23,951. Smallpox in children was said to be mild and rarely fatal. The disease increased irregularly throughout the eighteenth century, on average killing about 1,500 a year in London. But smallpox now was almost entirely a disease of early childhood, over 90% of deaths occurring under the age of five. As the disease dwindled in the nineteenth century (in London in 1837 it killed 217 people out of 21,063 total deaths) mainly due to vaccination, the proportion of cases in childhood diminished and those of young adults increased. Thus, in the early twentieth century, the disease had reached full circle having almost the same characteristics as when it first appeared in the early seventeenth century.

## INFANTILE DIARRHOEA

Infantile diarrhoea is still a dreaded disease in two-thirds of the world, where conditions are like those of the early nineteenth and early

* Creighton curiously did not believe in the germ theory of disease. The theory quoted is to be found in *The Natural History of Infectious Disease* (see Bibliography).

twentieth centuries in England and Wales. In Egypt, for example, infantile diarrhoea and enteritis still cause one third of *all* deaths—adult as well as infant—and in Greece, Portugal and Chile one in ten deaths are caused by this ailment.

Table 13 shows some figures of mortality from infantile diarrhoea in the mid and late nineteenth century in England and Wales.

## TABLE 13

*Annual deaths from infantile diarrhoea*

| 1866 | 18,266 | 1876 | 22,417 | 1886 | 24,748 |
|------|--------|------|--------|------|--------|
| 1867 | 20,813 | 1877 | 15,282 | 1887 | 20,242 |
| 1868 | 30,929 | 1878 | 25,103 | 1888 | 12,839 |
| 1869 | 20,775 | 1879 | 11,463 | 1889 | 18,434 |
| 1870 | 26,126 | 1880 | 30,185 | 1890 | 17,429 |
| 1871 | 24,937 | 1881 | 14,536 | 1891 | 13,962 |
| 1872 | 23,034 | 1882 | 17,185 | 1892 | 15,336 |
| 1873 | 22,514 | 1883 | 15,983 | 1893 | 28,755 |
| 1874 | 21,888 | 1884 | 26,412 | | |
| 1875 | 24,729 | 1885 | 13,398 | | |

These large annual totals stand almost wholly for deaths of infants.
From *A History of Epidemics in Britain*, C. Creighton, Cambridge, 1894.

From year to year the mortality fluctuated enormously, the rise and fall depending for the most part on the kind of summer. The summer of 1893 was hot and was accompanied by excessive mortality from infantile diarrhoea. In the main, three-quarters of the deaths were of infants in their first year. Middle life was fairly free from this cause of death but at 55 and upwards it became as fatal as it was in infancy. Here are some comparative figures from Logan. In 1848–72 the death-rate from diarrhoea and enteritis per million living of girls aged from one to four was 2,009, and in 1947 it was 94. At aged 65 and over the disease killed 2,479 per million in 1848–72; in 1947, 111. Compared with the United Kingdom, many countries are now over a century behind with respect to this disease.

# 19: Infectious Diseases—
a Changing Pattern

MEASLES, whooping cough and diphtheria are high on the list of 'catching' diseases in the world, that cause death. In 1963, 508,000 died from measles, 112,000 from whooping cough and 127,000 from diphtheria. Other figures include, 35,000 from polio and 6,000 from scarlet fever. Very likely most of these figures are underestimates.

Let us take some specific examples of changing patterns of disease in common ailments. Measles can be a serious disease today in the U.S.A. and Europe but it can be a terrible killer in Asia, Africa and South America where it attacks underfed populations who are living under primitive conditions and are not immune. In crowded areas in India, South America and Africa, fatality from measles is comparable with rates in England in the last century. In 1888 for example, an epidemic in Stoke on Trent alone caused 342 deaths. In 1848–72 the mean annual death-rate from measles of males, per million in England and Wales was 435, in 1947 it was 18 and in 1966, three altogether. Modern drugs and antibiotics have cut the death-rate in this particular country but it is still a serious enemy of man.

Whooping cough, like measles is a serious disease of children who are ill-fed. In 1837 it was third in the league table of killers of children, causing 3,044 deaths in six months, 1,066 of them in the London area. In Scotland in 1889, it caused 2,268 deaths. In 1848–72 in England and Wales the mean annual death-rate for males per million was 471; in 1947, 2, and in 1966 only one. Immunization against whooping cough has been used widely in the last 20 years.

In 1892, in London alone, diphtheria killed 3,196 people. In 1938 nearly 3,000 died, 2,744 being children. Extensive immunization against diphtheria was undertaken during the 1939–45 war with spectacular results. There were no deaths in 1965.

Scarlet fever was first described by Sydenham in 1676 when it was a mild disease. It became very serious in the late eighteenth century and again in the mid-nineteenth century. It was at its worst in 1863 when it caused the death of 30,475 people. In 1848–72 the mean death-rate per million of living males was 1,341; in 1947, one, in 1966, zero. Neither immunization nor vaccination can control the disease and sulphonamides which are effective against it were not introduced until 1932. The decline in severity of the disease before that date might have been due to a change in the virulence of the bacillus; it might have mutated to a milder form in the third quarter of the nineteenth century.

The diseases described above are rapidly acting and acutely infectious, resulting in death or recovery. Pulmonary tuberculosis (consumption) is an infectious disease of a more chronic nature. It takes third place today of diseases causing the most deaths in the world (the estimated figure is 2,800,000 which is probably a gross underestimate). In England and Wales the death-rate per million living for males was 2,532 in 1848–72; in 1966 it was 69 for all. Medical treatment had little to do with the fall up till twenty years ago when drugs were developed. The steady drop in death-rates was mainly caused by improvement in diet, less overcrowding and higher standards of health, in particular the prevention of spitting. And since 1943 the extensive use of mass radiography has done much to enable doctors to eliminate the disease at its earliest stages.

To give an idea of the *total* change in pattern in deaths in England and Wales from measles, whooping cough, diphtheria and scarlet fever; in 1861–70 of every million children under 15 about 6,000 died yearly from these diseases; in 1965 the number of deaths from these causes was only 11.

Fig. 24 shows the same picture in graph form.

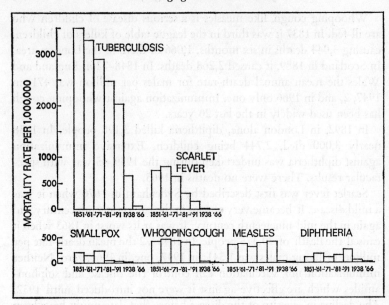

FIG. 24 Mean annual mortality rates in England and Wales due to certain communicable diseases. From McKeown and Record, *Population Studies*, XI.

# 20: Modern Epidemics—Adults

THE effective control of, or reduced mortality from, most infectious diseases like the above have been the main factors in enabling most of the population here and in other rich countries to live on into their second half-century so bringing other diseases into prominence. Money brings with it the ability to overeat (see Table 14), over-smoke, ride about in cars and use automatic machinery to do and finish jobs. All this affluence contributes to diseases of the heart and lungs: cancer of the lung, heart attack and stroke, chronic bronchitis. Such diseases, as pointed out in the companion volume,* are rare in hungry, technically backward countries because their inhabitants do not live long enough as yet to be attacked by degenerative disease. These people live to about the age of fifty on average, and are at the same stage as our grandfathers were in 1900.

## HEART ATTACK, STROKE, CANCERS

Fig. 25 shows the proportion of male to female deaths, from cancer, heart and circulatory disease and from accidents in England and Wales,

*Biology and the Social Crisis.*

## TABLE 14

*Weight and Death*

| Principal causes of death among men rated overweight, aged 25–74 | | Principal causes of death among women rated overweight, aged 25–74 | |
|---|---|---|---|
| Cause of death | Increased percentage of risk | Cause of death | Increased percentage of risk |
| Principal cardiovascular-renal diseases: | 49 | Principal cardiovascular-renal diseases | 77 |
| Organic heart disease, diseases of the coronary arteries and angina pectoris | | Organic heart disease, diseases of the coronary arteries and angina pectoris | 75 |
| | 42 | Cerebral haemorrhage | 62 |
| Cerebral haemorrhage | 59 | Chronic nephritis | 112 |
| Chronic nephritis | 91 | Cancer: | |
| Cancer: | | Liver and gall bladder | 111 |
| Liver and gall bladder | 68 | Peritoneum, intestines and rectum | 4 |
| Peritoneum, intestines and rectum | 15 | Pancreas | 49 |
| Diabetes | 283 | Genital organs | 7 |
| Pneumonia | 2 | Uterus | 21 |
| Cirrhosis of the liver | 49 | Leukemia and Hodgkin's | 10 |
| Appendicitis | 123 | Diabetes | 272 |
| Hernia and intestinal obstruction | 54 | Pneumonia | 29 |
| Biliary calculi and other gall bladder diseases: | 52 | Cirrhosis of the liver | 47 |
| Biliary calculi | 106 | Appendicitis | 95 |
| Accidents | 11 | Hernia and intestinal obstruction | 41 |
| Car accidents | 31 | Biliary calculi and other gall bladder diseases: | 88 |
| Falls | 31 | Biliary calculi | 184 |
| | | Puerperal conditions | 62 |
| Cause of death | Decreased percentage of risk | Accidents | 35 |
| | | Car accidents | 20 |
| Cancer, all forms: | 3 | | |
| Stomach | 15 | Cause of death | Decreased percentage of risk |
| Pancreas | 7 | | |
| Respiratory organs | 22 | Cancer: | |
| Tuberculosis | 79 | Stomach | 14 |
| Ulcer of stomach and duodenum | 33 | Breast | 31 |
| Suicide | 22 | Tuberculosis | 65 |
| | | Suicide | 17 |

The fatter you are, the shorter your life will be. The death rate goes up by 13 per cent for every 10 per cent, an individual exceeds the ideal weight for his build. On average, the mortality rate rises from approximately 1½ times the expected rate for people up to 45 per cent overweight to nearly three times the expected rate for those who are 60 to 74 per cent overweight. This excess mortality is largely accounted for by the high death rates from the degenerative diseases of the heart, arteries and kidneys; diabetes; and certain disorders of the

(*continued on foot of page 122*)

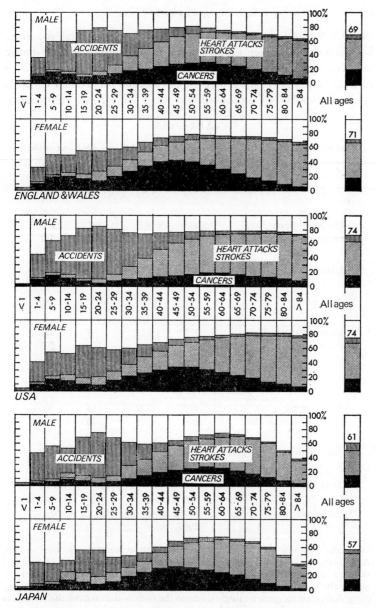

FIG. 25 Cancer and cardiovascular diseases. Deaths from cancers, heart attacks, strokes and accidents (percentage of total mortality per age group, by sex, 1962–3). From De Haas in *Health of Mankind* (ed. G. Wolstenholme), Churchill, 1967.

the U.S.A. and Japan in 1962-3. It is clear that in all these countries, both in men and women, the proportion of heart and circulatory disease increases with age. At the age of 40–44 for men, 30 to 40% (Japan 22%) of total mortality is caused by these diseases and for women 15–25%. At the age of 70–74 the proportion is about half for men and women.

TABLE 15A

*Leading causes of death in middle age in England and Wales 1965 (per million)*

|  | Males | | Females | |
| --- | --- | --- | --- | --- |
|  | 45–54 | 55–64 | 45–54 | 55–64 |
| Coronary heart | 2,435 | 6,800 | 391 | 1,794 |
| Other cardio vascular | 578 | 1,796 | 481 | 1,257 |
| Strokes | 460 | 1,740 | 388 | 1,334 |
| All cancer | 2,040 | 6,115 | 1,998 | 3,640 |
| Bronchitis | 351 | 1,824 | 97 | 315 |
| Pneumonia | 148 | 519 | 100 | 293 |
| Suicide | 185 | 256 | 141 | 180 |
| Motor traffic | 175 | 222 | 68 | 106 |
| Other violent death | 200 | 279 | 75 | 132 |
| All other causes | 791 | 1,885 | 618 | 1,274 |
| Total deaths | 7,363 | 21,436 | 4,357 | 10,325 |

From Logan, R. F. L., Health Hazards, *Middle Age*, B.B.C. publications, 1967.

liver, biliary tract and bowels. These causes of death were not always so important. As recently as the 1930s, insurance companies gave preferential rates to anyone who was slightly overweight, as the great killer then was tuberculosis, and this is one of the handful of deaths you are less likely to meet if you are overweight. Now diabetes is the greatest single threat to the obese—deaths from this condition are approximately four times higher than average for people who are overweight. One interesting feature is the significant and constant low mortality ratio from suicide which is found in both overweight men and women. Though the outlook for them may be grim, they seem to prove a short life can still be a merry one.
From *Sunday Times Colour Supplement, March 16th 1969.*

## TABLE 15B

*Cancer deaths in middle age in England and Wales 1965 (per million)*

|  | Males | | Females | |
|  | *45–54* | *55–64* | *45–54* | *55–64* |
| --- | --- | --- | --- | --- |
| **Lung** | | | | |
| Primary | 624 | 2,066 | 142 | 269 |
| Unspecified | 262 | 872 | 64 | 120 |
| *Breast* | 1 | 8 | 577 | 824 |
| Uterus cervix | — | — | 191 | 200 |
|    other | — | — | 57 | 139 |
| Ovary and tubes | — | — | 219 | 315 |
| Prostate | 22 | 162 | — | — |
| Bladder | 52 | 212 | 18 | 52 |
| *Stomach* | 243 | 785 | 98 | 301 |
| Colon | 102 | 303 | 128 | 322 |
| Rectum | 79 | 251 | 57 | 160 |
| Brain and C.N.S. | 78 | 139 | 52 | 77 |
| Blood lymphatic | 143 | 273 | 90 | 185 |
| Other cancer | 434 | 1,044 | 305 | 676 |
| *All cancer* | 2,040 | 6,115 | 1,998 | 3,640 |

Cancer, by contrast to coronary heart disease which is a new epidemic, has taken a very steady toll of lives over the past 40 years. The static number of deaths conceals various changing patterns of death from cancers: within the past 10 years the fall in death-rates from stomach cancer, gut and rectum have been offset by a rise in cancers of the lung, blood, pancreas and bladder of men and women and in ovaries in women and prostate in men. Cancer of the breast has scarcely changed its toll of women over the past 40 years.

From Logan R. F. L., *op. cit.*

At the age of 50–54 cancers are responsible for 20–30% of total deaths in men and for 30–50% in women. In both sexes these percentages decrease with age. Together cancers and heart and circulatory diseases make up two-thirds of the total deaths in both sexes in the U.S.A. and in England and Wales; in Japan, half. From all this evidence it is reasonable to say that heart disease, stroke and cancer are the major killers in technologically developed regions (Table 15A and B).

Another 'disease' of rich countries is accidents. It is a male disease as the graphs show and the common age of death is 15–25.

One of the most serious aspects of coronary thrombosis is that it is spreading rapidly to younger and younger age groups as Fig. 26 shows.

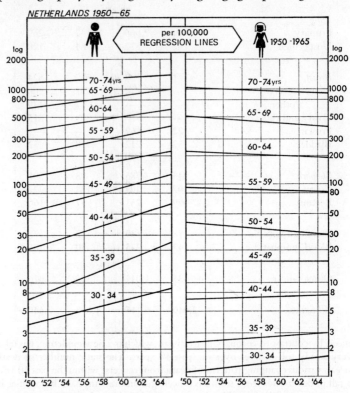

FIG. 26 Mortality from coronary thrombosis. This shows that deaths in men particularly have become more widespread in younger age groups. i.e. 25 deaths per 10,000 in 1965 compared with about seven in 1950 in the age group 35–39. From De Haas (See Fig. 25).

The disease emerged from obscurity during the early years of the century, particularly after the 1914–18 war. In men of all ages Logan reckons that in 1901–10, 34 per million living died from the disease, in 1921, 41, in 1931, 238 and in 1947, 1,222. Now, one in five develop coronary thrombosis in middle age.

Lung cancer too is a modern 'epidemic'. Lung cancer rates per 100,000 in England and Wales were 3 in 1911–15 and 57 in 1960–1 for men aged 45–49; and 7 and 361 respectively for men of 60–64. These epidemics are every bit as serious as the plagues of the past. If stroke, heart attack and lung cancer are represented as a black dot for each 1,000 deaths, and the dots are plotted over Europe and North America, both continents are covered in a cloak of darkness, just as bad as the plagues of old. Perhaps in half a century India will have changed her present cloak of disease for ours now unless the causes of degenerative diseases are discovered soon.

But have we an inkling of the causes of the rising graphs of thrombosis and lung cancer?

Cigarette smoking is, without doubt, a direct cause of lung cancer and is a culprit too in causing thrombosis. Air pollution by coal smoke, exhaust fumes and industrial effluents may play their part too in causing lung cancer. The evidence suggests this in some cases but not all. There is no increased mortality in long-distance lorry drivers who must breathe in more exhaust fumes than most of us. Then lung cancer deaths are high in Finland where the air is clear. And to mix up the picture still further, Japan with intense air pollution, has a low rate of lung cancer. The problem of the relationship between air pollution and lung cancer has not yet been cracked. And it has not even been chipped as far as the causes of coronary thrombosis are concerned, except to say that the causes seem to be multiple; somehow, for some people, related to heredity, diet, exercise, cigarette smoking and indeed patterns of behaviour (smoking, inactivity) found far back in childhood or adolescence. As in most ecological puzzles the single cause idea is suspect. For example, animal fats eaten in excess have been suggested as a cause of coronary thrombosis and the fact that both the number of coronaries and fat consumption fell in Norway during the war and rose after the war, as the usual Western diet was resumed, seemed to clinch the hypothesis. But there were other factors involved: total food intake was reduced, not just fats, average weight fell, people used their legs more, cigarettes were rare. To isolate a fat diet as the single cause from a tangle of other variables is impossible. Exercise is another imponderable in heart disease. It would be useful to know that if people did *not* take some form of exercise (even if they were thin and felt well) then they would be running the risk of having a coronary in later life. Circumstantial evidence like the higher rate of heart disease among sedentary clerks than among walking postmen points to a link between lack of exercise and heart disease. But other factors are entangled with exercise and serve to fog the issue: high blood pressure, cigarette smoking, heredity and so on and the weight of these factors will vary from individual to individual. Anyhow people differ, as we have stated in Chapter 4. One man's meat is another man's poison; some people keep fit because of exercise, some in spite of it. Perhaps we need to think of coronary thrombosis ecologically; that is of a complex interaction between men and their diverse ways of life. But whether this approach will lead to a theory based on the recognition of 'at risk' types for practical application remains to be seen.

## THE RISE AND FALL OF THE ULCER

Lung cancer and coronary thrombosis hit the headlines now for modern epidemic diseases of men but other internal diseases have been epidemic and have declined. Perhaps coronary thrombosis may gradually stop killing at the rate it is doing today. Duodenal ulcer reached epidemic proportions in the 1930s and 1940s and a survey in London after the war showed that by the time they were fifty-five about 6% of men, had or had had, a duodenal ulcer. Recently and without warning it has declined. In 1961 only about nine men aged 45–64 in 100,000 died of duodenal ulcer; in 1936–8 on average it caused the death of 17. Why is not known. There may have been a drop in the frequency of the disease, or a reduction in its severity or character which has made it more amenable to treatment. Do stresses now cause coronary thrombosis and not ulcer for some? The decline bristles with questions as does the rise in the rate of other diseases.

# 21: Modern Epidemics—Children

HERE in Britain and in most rich countries the scourge of infectious disease is a bogey of the past. So is rheumatic fever and other forms of heart disease, which killed 526 children in England and Wales aged 5 to 14 in 1938 but only 26 in 1965. Pneumonia, too, does not take the toll of lives it did. In 1938, 634 of the 5 to 14 year olds died; in 1965, 133. In the same period, death from appendicitis fell from 370 to 31; for diabetes, from 69 to 16; epilepsy, from 129 to 48 and surprisingly violence, including accidents from 1,230 to 914 (the largest single cause of death). And it is not only death-rates from the potentially fatal diseases which have fallen. The incidence of disease from impetigo, ringworm and scabies, not so long ago rampant among schoolchildren, has dropped also, thanks to the vigilance of many people and, of course, cleaner homes. Here are the relevant statistics for impetigo: in 1947 the number of children in England and Wales treated at clinics for this disease amounted to 67,129 but in 1966 it was only 6,306.

What has replaced these 'old' diseases? Now infectious and parasitic diseases cause only three per cent of deaths of children between 5 and 14. Of the 2,556 deaths of 5 to 14 year olds in 1965 accidents accounted for 36%, cancer (including leukaemia) 20%, congenital malformations for 10%, and respiratory disease (asthma and pneumonia) for 8%. Of the 19,060 deaths under five, congenital malformations and respiratory disease (mainly pneumonia) each claimed 19%; accidents came next with 7% and were followed by infections and parasitic diseases, enteritis and cancer each accounting for 2% of the total.

Deaths are only the tip of the iceberg. Children who suffer from many physical and mental handicaps and who would have died 50 years ago either of infectious disease or because no operation had been devised to save them, are now alive. There are for example about 3,000 spastics in special schools; nearly half are educationally subnormal and the hearing of a fifth is defective. And as if this was not enough, they may have severe speech and language disorders and some are emotionally disturbed. Then another 'epidemic' is that of spina bifida. Rather less than two per 1,000 babies born alive have this condition, of which 90% used to die in infancy. Thanks to an operation devised in 1950, and improved medical and nursing care nearly half survive beyond the age of five. But skilled medical and nursing care is needed beyond their school days. Harelip, cleft palate and pyloric stenosis are also on the increase, as are blindness and partial sight, biochemical diseases like phenylketonuria, deafness and partial deafness, and speech disorders. Many of these new diseases will have a genetic component. Diabetes is caused by many genes, others by specific major genes: haemophilia and phenylketonuria for example. Others are caused by chromosome defects. In advanced countries it has been calculated that 6% of liveborn children carry genetic or chromosome defects. This 6% of abnormalities can be broken down as follows:

> 1%: chromosomes and pieces of chromosomes (for example, mongolism)
> 1%: specific major genes (for example, phenylketonuria)
> 4%: unidentified 'polygenes' (for example, diabetes)

These defects are in a strict sense incurable: if the carrier reproduces they are liable to be handed down to all succeeding generations. And now they can reproduce, because they can be saved, by cure or palliative treatment. In later generations therefore the frequency of these genetic diseases will mount; parents who have been saved will bring into the world children who will be likewise saved.

In poor countries, in Asia, Africa and Latin America doctors are still battling away with the 'old' diseases of tuberculosis, typhoid, measles, diphtheria, severe malnutrition and others. Speech and language disorders are noted, but nothing much can be done about them simply because of a shortage of medical man power; and anyway they appear as trifles compared with the many gross and grave physical illnesses. A few figures to underline the point. Combined death-rates from the four common ailments of childhood—whooping cough, diphtheria, measles and scarlet fever—per 100,000 in 1961–2 were: England and Wales 0·2; the U.S.A., 0·3; Mexico 33·8; Chile 39·0; Guatemala 147.

# 22: The Eight Ages of Man

WHAT are the major patterns of death in the main ages of western man? The eight diagrams (Fig. 27) summarize the main trends. We will select a few main points from these. First, as we have seen, infant mortality (deaths under one year) have declined due to a reduction in deaths from diseases such as gastro-enteritis and broncho-pneumonia. But the gap between the death-rates from poor and better-off homes persists (see Fig. 22). At pre-school age (1–4 years) the infectious diseases have lost their power to kill due to medical advance. But pneumonia, cancers, accidents, congenital malformations take their toll. At school age (5–14) death-rates are low and at adolescence and after (15–24) the 'social' diseases—accidents and suicide—begin to bite. With the young adult (25–34) too, road accidents cause many deaths and suicide rates increase. At the adult stage (35–44) the different patterns of disease of men and women begin to emerge. In men, coronary thrombosis begins to show itself and the socially preventable disease, lung cancer. And in women, cancer of the cervix starts to kill, perhaps another social phenomenon in that it is possibly preventable by cleanliness — there is some evidence that the disease increases with decreasing economic standards. Middle age

**A.** *0-1 year old infants.* Rapid decline in infant mortality, especially aged one month to one year, but small improvement in the first month. Decline in death-rate due to reduction in deaths from gastro-enteritis, broncho-pneumonia. Gap between death-rates of rich and poor still with us.

**B.** *1-4 years old. Pre-school age.* Big improvement in death-rate with the control of infectious diseases: diptheria, measles, whooping cough and tuberculosis. Pneumonia still a notable cause of death with malformations, accidents and cancers. Leukaemia, the cancers and congenital heart defects have increased.

**H.** *65 +. Older ages.* The patterns of middle life are broadly continued. Analysis of what people die of more difficult because of inadequacies of certification and complexity of the death entries. Men die before women on average.

**G.** *45-64 years old. Middle life.* Commonest causes of death in both sexes are coronary thrombosis, stroke, cancers, pneumonia and bronchitis. In men the prominent cancer is of the lung; in women, the breast.

Fig. 27 What People die of from the cradle to old age.

C. *5-14 years old. School age.* Lowest death-rates of any age mainly because of eradication of infectious diseases and rheumatic fever. Deaths from cancers increasing slowly and from congenital heart disease quickly. Deaths from road accidents not increasing but twice as many boys as girls are killed in this way.

D. *15-24 years old. Adolescence and after.* Road accidents account for nearly half the deaths and five times as many men as women are killed in this way. Tuberculosis used to be a serious killer but not now. Suicide rates have gone up and down in men but are always higher than in women, where they have been rising for some years.

F. *35-44 years old. Adult.* Divergence between men and women more marked. In men coronary thrombosis, lung cancer and suicide prominent. In women breast cancer, cancer of the neck of the womb and suicide. But in general death rates are low.

E. *25-34 years old. Young adult.* Causes of death in men and women start to diverge. Road accidents and suicides are the main causes of death and have been rising for both sexes. Suicide rates have risen since the 1950's.

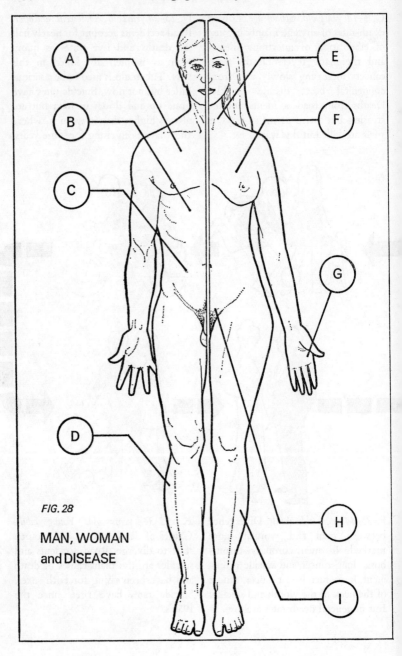

*FIG. 28*

**MAN, WOMAN
and DISEASE**

FIG. 28 Man, Woman and Diseases (England and Wales).

A. *Chronic bronchitis:* males predominate in ratio of 3 : 2. Asthma: twice as frequent in men as in women.

B. *Lung cancer:* deaths from cancer of the lung are thought to be a key factor in the striking lack of improvement in the death-rate for middle-aged men over the last half century. In 1966, 22,600 men and 4,400 women died from lung cancer. Smoking is likely to be a prominent cause.

C. *Ulcers:* until puberty, females are as liable as males. Ulcers then become more common in both sexes, but four times as common in males. After the menopause, the incidence rises in women. Duodenal ulcer is 10 times more common in men.

D. *Muscular dystrophy:* like colour blindness and haemophilia (pathological excess bleeding from wounds), it is almost exclusively a male disease, but is transmitted by women through a sex-linked defective gene. Through her children Queen Victoria passed on haeomophilia to Spanish and Russian royal families.

E. *Thyroid* disease occurs much more frequently in women.

F. *Breast cancer:* 10,000 deaths each year, of which one per cent are men. Doctors stress the importance of not ignoring a strange lump in the breast, for early treatment is nearly always successful.

G. *Rheumatoid arthritis:* three times as common in women.

H. *Cystitis:* this irritating inflammation of the bladder has been dubbed 'miniskirtitis' recently by some doctors as it is on the increase in women who wear miniskirts. The bladder is able to 'catch cold' more easily, these doctors claim.

I. *Varicose veins:* a common complaint amongst women and accentuated in many by the extra weight of pregnancy. In some women varicose veins are more troublesome during the menstrual cycle.

After *The Observer* Colour Supplement. For further details about diseases of men and women see Tables 15A and B.

(45–64) intensifies the patterns of the adult stage; heart attack, stroke and cancers are the common forms of death. Old age (65+) continues the patterns of middle life.

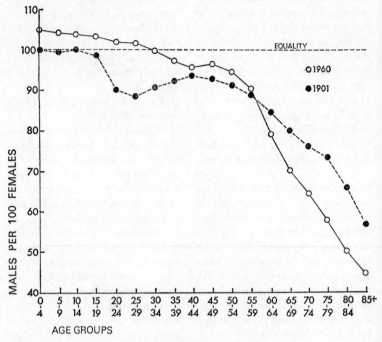

FIG. 29 Sex-ratio according to age (England and Wales).

Fig. 28 summarizes some common diseases of men and women. A glance at Fig. 8 shows how different these are from those suffered by men and women in under-developed countries. Fig. 29 shows the sex-ratio according to age in 1960 and 1901. It indicates that the progress of medicine has preserved more males than females well into adult life (up to ages 25–29); after this, but especially after 55, to be female is in itself an advantage.

# 23: Is Health Improving?

AN absurd question? What do we mean by health? If we take it to mean, as it is defined by the World Health Organization, 'a state of complete physical, mental and social well being and not merely the absence of disease or infirmity', we shall be searching for the unattainable, 'a will o' the wisp luring its followers into the swamps of unreality'. Indeed most of us, on this definition are ill. The standard of 'health' from one country to another and within a country differs; perhaps in India a man can drive his bullocks all day long with a headache and diarrhoea and still be happy, while many of us here would be at the doctor's surgery. As individuals too, we must feel different. One man's standard of mental and social well being may not be acceptable to another.

How do we then obtain an indicator of health? Perhaps only by the hard evidence of death-rates and the crude indicators of health—infant mortality and longevity, which show that people are living longer and not nearly so many babies die, as say in 1900. If these are used as our measuring rod then we are becoming healthier (but note that the suicide rate is increasing and this may be an indicator of the mental health of a country).

Illness as opposed to death is often unquantifiable and only sometimes measurable. As ways of life change and research discovers cures, so do health problems. We have noted this in the previous chapters; the plague has vanished here but lung cancer is with us. What you lose on the swings you gain on the roundabouts. The reality about health is that, in an ever-changing world each period and each civilization will continue to bear its burden of disease created by an unavoidable failure to adapt to the new environment.

# Part 5: Migration: The Brain and Brawn Drain

Part 5: Migration: The Brain
and Brawn Drain

# 24: Migration and the Biologist

EVERY animal we know about, except man, is to some extent
a professional in its own niche in the environment. Usually it
is confined to a limited geographical area—its range, because
it requires a certain group of favourable conditions in order to survive
and make its living. Maybe it has a limited range of tolerance to temperature, or certain fixed requirements for food or certain essentials
for breeding purposes—nest building and so on. Man stands apart here.
He is, as Chapter 5 showed, the amateur of the animal kingdom. His
body machinery, particularly his temperature-controlling process, has
helped him to break through the barriers of heat, cold, drought and
the thin air of mountains. But without the backing of an enormous
genetic diversity, a superb brain and versatile hands, he would not have
gone far. Fire, clothing, shelter, foods and of course speech are prog-
enies of the brain and these as we have seen, have fed back on the brain
to improve it continually in a one-way direction. Because of all these
gifts, physical and mental, man has been able to do what no other
animal could do and spread over the whole globe into every niche.

We have learned in Chapter 7 something of the two very early
expansionary migrations of men of half a million years and 40,000

years ago. The first no doubt was animal-like, to search for new food sources and to avoid inclement weather, but nevertheless, driven by an exploratory and developing brain. It is unlikely that either migration was strongly directed by the 'currency of an idea' as were the later religious and political migrations or expulsions. Neither was likely to be *selective*. Migrations of this type began when a definite social structure had developed. When the Sea Empire of Crete collapsed in about 1470 B.C. it was the governing and technical classes who moved to where the living was better (Chapter 15). The modest farmers, it seems, were left behind to till the olive groves. When Constantinople fell to the Turks in 1453 it extinguished a civilization that had lasted 1,000 years. It also caused a migration of minds which helped to renew Western civilization and to help the West after many centuries to recapture the whole world for itself. In other words the loss was selective and there was a brain-drain.

On a humbler level, but no less important, Vernon in 1951 noticed that British service-men, classed as migrants had higher I.Q. scores than those who were not. 'Home-keeping youth have ever homely wits', Shakespeare says appropriately. And, as far as the vast majority of coloured immigrants into this country is concerned, they must have enterprise. It takes a good deal of initiative for a farm labourer to leave his familiar village and travel by air to London and seek work there or in other large cities.

In the next chapter, then, we shall consider how and why migration can modify the character of the two communities involved, the loser and the gainer. Particularly we shall look at the genetically determined qualities of fertility and 'intelligence'. In Chapter 27 we shall see how the expulsion of the Jews and the Huguenots from Spain and from France affected those countries and in Chapters 29 and 30 we shall examine how the inherited blood genes can help to answer the questions 'Who are the English?', 'Who are the Jews?'

# 25: Exodus of Muscle and Talent

WHAT causes people to migrate? Better land; the draw of a bigger town; the magnet of a metropolis, like London, or Paris, or Rome, where wealth and power attract ability and enterprise from the provinces; or, as we know, by the flight of talent from Britain, the glitter of another land entirely. In most of these cases a brain-drain is set up by people 'seeking their fortunes' or more modestly moving to where living and work are better. For society, migration (or expulsion) is important because genetic potential goes with the migrants if they are young enough to breed. 'Intelligence', as Sir Cyril Burt and many other have concluded, 'when adequately assessed is largely dependent upon genetic constitution'. Not upon single genes, but upon many, each producing small 'plus or minus effects', see the footnote on page 27.

## IRELAND AND LOSS OF FERTILITY

Between 1815 and 1914, Great Britain lost at least 20 million people by migration. The end of the Napoleonic wars, failure of harvests, a rapid increase in population—the effect of a falling death-rate with continued high fertility—caused some population pressure and led certain people to look to the New World for a better life. About 13 of the 20 million went to the States, four to Canada and one and a half to Australia. This was no brain-drain. Most of the migrants were agricultural and unskilled workers—the very ablest men, as Galton noted were strongly discouraged from emigrating from England, preferring 'to live in the high intellectual and moral atmosphere of the more intellectual circles of English society, to a self-banishment among people of altogether lower grades of mind and interests'.

If England was not noticeably altered by the drain, Ireland was. The background to the Irish migrations was a failure in the star-crop of the country—the potato. When this crop was introduced in Ireland in 1754, the population stood at 3,200,000. In less than a century it had leaped to 8,175,000 (1846). But in 1845 and succeeding years disaster came. The crop, mainstay of flesh and blood, was blighted by a fungal disease. In 1845 a third to a half of the crop was lost. In 1846 it was again destroyed suddenly. July 12th saw the crop healthy; a night or two later a foodless people wrung their hands over a rotting waste of vegetation. The threat of starvation forced an 'animal-like' migration from Ireland on a vast scale. Between 1845-7 about a million went to the States and a similar number to England and Wales. In one week in 1847, 130,000 Irish paupers descended on Liverpool; Glasgow was similarly inundated. Kerry, Cork and Mayo were the counties the hardest hit. In 1851 the population was down to 5,112,000; by 1871 it had sunk to 4,053,000, half the peak number. The exodus was largely from the land. And it was the young, and therefore fertile, who left and still do to this day. In 1880, for example, over half those who emigrated to the States were between 15 and 24 years old and a further quarter between 25 and 44. In 1920 the picture had not changed much; two thirds were between 15 and 24 and a further quarter of the older age-group. Most were unmarried and, atypically, the women outnumbered the men—and still do. In 1946-51, 1,397 women emigrated for every 1,000 men; a total of 120,000 emigrated. In 1956-61, 212,000 went. The drain, of course, left the older and therefore less fertile people at home. Indeed the offspring of fertile families were more likely to have greater pressures put on them to emigrate.

What was (and is) the effect on Ireland? Selective migration appears to have modified the character of the people in many respects. Marriages, partly for social reasons are late and few. But the intensive emigration may have selectively lowered the fertility of the people who remained and this may have led to the uniquely low and stable birth-rate in Ireland today which has for nearly a century remained at much less than half the peak number (2,818,314 in the 1961 census). This statement, of course, remains a theory until there is evidence of a low fertility of married people compared with similar age groups in England or elsewhere.

## THE EFFECT OF IMMIGRATION ON THE UNITED STATES

The diversity and magnitude of the immigrant streams to America, from the early religious pioneers to the Irish, prevented any single group from becoming ascendant and establishing a strong governing class in that country. This classlessness remains today. Freedom of movement, of job and of religion have produced in the United States a more frequent hybridization perhaps than has ever been known before in human history, producing perhaps the exuberance and instability, characteristic of the American people (see Chapter 11).

Migrations to the States, as elsewhere, have revealed an instinctive, genetic characteristic of men: a search for environments as similar to those of their ancestral homes as they could find. Basically it was a problem of adaptation to ecological conditions, both geographical and cultural. Thus, the Scandinavians and Finns settled round the northern lakes. The Italians took wine-growing to California. Greeks and Lebanese, hardened traders, went to places where they could be involved in commerce. Chinese, often from the same province, went to where they could find success as cooks and launderers. Craftsmen like Cornish miners, went as they always have done, straight to mining areas in Nevada, Colorado and Wisconsin. Meanwhile the Jews, unhampered by persecution, could develop their skills in law, medicine and mathematics. While there was hybridization between these groups (and this was a force that welded the people together) it was not, and is not, a freely interbreeding society. The mixture has settled in different patterns: it has separated out into communities which by some inbreeding preserve the culture and genetic character which would vanish by free inter-marriage.

## MASS EXODUS OF TALENT FROM BRITAIN

Let us turn to some modern evidence. We know that at present there is a steady emigration of graduates from this country to America, Canada and Australia. In 1966 alone the number of engineers who emigrated was equivalent to 42% of the annual output of the universities. In the case of scientists it was 23%. On present trends, about 100,000 graduates (not all scientists and engineers) will have emigrated between 1960–70. The drain is causing the pool of talent in the middle classes to sink steadily lower and lower. Why? Because one of the effects of the inheritance of a high I.Q. in a society like our own, is that gifted people can rise in the social system. These talented strains tend to become established in the middle class where for some decades now the reproductive rate has been lower than that of the working class (although it is now increasing slightly as explained in Chapter 2). Thus, not only is the proportion of inherited talent on the decline, but the decline is accelerated by the brain drain. Richard Lynn has calculated that the loss is about one third of the universities' annual output, taking the engineers and scientists together. If talent in all its forms is inherited, and all evidence suggests that it is, and assuming that each graduate has but one son (the average size of British middle-class families is less than two) then in the next generation to enter the universities in the 1990s there will only be two-thirds of the number of talented young men there are today. The reduction would not be quite so great as this because all the time, highly intelligent children are emerging from 'average' parents, while some highly intelligent parents have only averagely intelligent children.

This rapid leak of talent is serious. As in past ages (Chapter 15) the economic prosperity of this and all civilized countries depends on a few thousand key men. Probably only 5,000 key business men control industry and commerce in Britain. And the maintenance of high standards in other spheres—medicine, the law, education, administration, depends likewise on a few thousand gifted individuals. The loss of a third of the families which produce talent (i.e. the scientific and engineering talents) may well reduce standards in the next few generations. A vicious circle will begin: massive exodus of talent, declining living standards leading to more loss of talent. Richard Lynn suggests that, 'The competence of the population could in time decline to the level of that of the Eskimos and the Red Indians and British civilization become extinct.'

NHM—L

# 26: Selective Migration within Britain

SELECTIVE migration is revealed not only in the departure of people *from* Britain but also in the movement of population *within* the country. We know that there is much variation in the average intellectual abilities of populations in various parts of the country. Table 16 shows the IQ league table of 1951. In it the Home counties lead (mean IQ 104·0), with London about middle (100·6) and Glasgow and South-West Scotland bottom (93·7). Selective migration may have helped to produce these variations (which probably underestimate the real variations of the areas concerned) for migrants have a mean IQ of 102·8 and natives 99·0.

Some information exists about the relationship between IQ scores and population change in various County Boroughs and is set out in the chart (Fig. 31). But it should be pointed out that population change may *not* have been entirely due to migration but to other factors—higher birth-rates or lower death-rates for example. What is interesting is that where population declined, for whatever reason, from 1931–51, as in Smethwick or Salford, the mean IQ at 11+ was lower than when its population increased, as in Bournemouth or Darlington. More data

TABLE 16

*Mean scores of Servicemen from different areas of Britain (Vernon, 1951)*

| Region of Great Britain | Numbers | Mean Score |
|---|---|---|
| Home Counties | 1,663 | 104·0 |
| East Anglia, Beds, Cambs, Northants | 474 | 101·7 |
| S.W. and Hants | 563 | 101·5 |
| Berks, Bucks, Oxon, Glos, Hereford, Worcs | 540 | 101·4 |
| Leics, Notts, Derby, Yorks W., Cheshire | 1,128 | 101·4 |
| London | 695 | 100·6 |
| Yorks E. & N., Northumberland, Durham, Cumberland | 502 | 99·6 |
| Scotland E. and N. Counties | 486 | 99·6 |
| Wales | 466 | 97·9 |
| Lancashire | 1,125 | 97·2 |
| Warwick, Staffs, Salop | 1,046 | 97·1 |
| Glasgow and S.W. Scotland | 495 | 93·7 |
|  | % |  |
| Natives | 74·8 | 99·0 |
| Migrants | 25·2 | 102·8 |

From 'Regional variations in intellectual ability in Britain', by J. A. H. Lee, *Eugenics Review,* **49**, 1, 1957.

is needed, however, to substantiate the hypothesis that selective migration is an important cause of variation in the average intelligence of different populations.

Greater probability is given to this hunch by considering standards of farming in relation to migration. Population movements on the land bear witness to the well-established tendency noted by Dudley Stamp, 'That the poor farmer tends to gravitate to the poor farm and the poor land; the good man makes good on good land and seeks more and better land.' Little research has been done here on this matter but this 'law' surely applies.

We know that people have migrated from the land in England, Scotland and Wales and the maps in Fig. 30 starkly record the story for about half a century. In the main mechanization and low wages have driven men off the land to the cities. Would the IQ map reveal in Britain a similar story to that of Tasmania where research has established the correlation, poor land lower IQ, better land higher IQ?

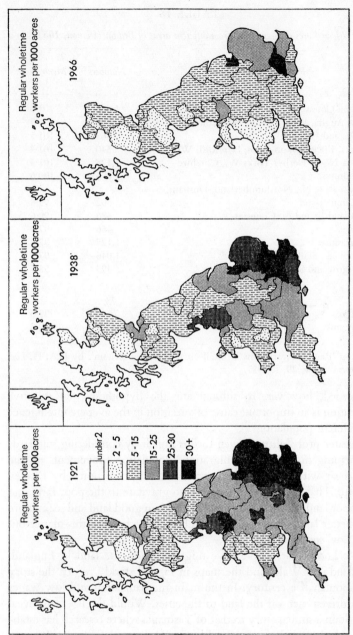

FIG. 30 How men have left the land: three maps from the Ministry of Agriculture's *A Century of Agricultural Statistics*.

Regular wholetime workers per 1000 acres

1921

under 2
2 - 5
5 - 15
15 - 25
25 - 30
30 +

Regular wholetime workers per 1000 acres

1938

Regular wholetime workers per 1000 acres

1966

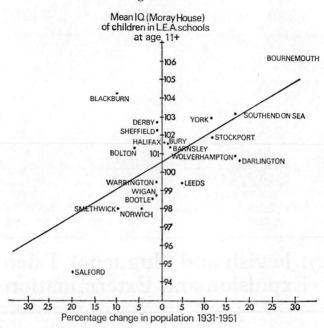

FIG. 31 The relationship between the intelligence of school-children in a series of English County Boroughs and the changes in population in these over the last twenty years. From 'Regional Variations in Intellectual Ability in Britain' J. A. H. Lee, *Eugenics Review*, 49, 1957.

# 27: Jewish and Huguenot Talent : Expulsion and Extermination

## THE JEWS

GALTON, writing in 1869 of the Spanish described them as 'superstitious' and 'unintelligent' and put this down to the drain of free thinkers by martyrdom and imprisonment during the Spanish Inquisition. The Spanish Inquisition was established in 1478 when the King of Spain was authorized by Papal Bull to control the persecution and conviction and execution of heretics against the Church. This destruction or imprisonment of genetic potential for over three centuries was not, of course, migration, but it had the same effect as a brain drain. It was almost certainly added to by the expulsion of the Jews who having been in Spain since A.D. 140 were expelled in 1492 and 1496.

Between 1478 and 1781, the main period of the Inquisition, Galton reckons that Spain was drained of talent by death and imprisonment at the rate of a 1,000 a year; on average 100 executed and 900 imprisoned. The actual data during the 300 years are: 32,000 burnt, and 291,000 condemned to various terms of imprisonment and other penalties.

The number of well-to-do literate Jews who refused to conform and were expelled in the twenty years following 1492, amounted to 90,000. These exiled Spanish Jews were called the Sephardim or 'the people from afar'. But 50,000 'converted' Jews stayed in Spain. They were named *marranos* (pigs). Watched and persecuted, banned from all offices of profit and honour these poorer Jews and their descendants were marked men. (As early as 1215 Pope Innocent III ordered all Jews to wear a yellow badge to distinguish them.) Such an intolerable position forced further migration and a stream of *marranos* left Spain. In fact, their 'conversion' proved to be short-lived and they settled largely in Antwerp and Amsterdam contributing to the cultural and commercial glories of the Netherlands in the Seventeenth and Eighteenth Centuries.

Of the unconverted Jews 45,000 (about half) went to Turkey, 15,000 to North Africa and Egypt and the remainder to Southern France and Holland, Northern Italy, South America, Jamaica and elsewhere. Bajazet II, Ottoman Sultan in Turkey, forecast that the Jews would enrich him and impoverish Spain. He was proved right. They settled in Constantinople, Salonika and Smyrna. Later they followed the Turks to Palestine and Egypt. In these countries they provided the professional classes needed by the young Empire as a substitute for the Christian Greeks.

In summary, as Darlington puts it, Spain lost more with the expulsion of the Jews than she gained with her Empire in the Indies. 'Her decay proceeded step by step with the suppression of heresy and infidelity and the hunting out of the Jews. Spain never recovered from the loss of the Jews.'*

Since the original migrations of Jews from Ancient Palestine sixty or seventy generations have encountered internal insurrections, brutal massacres, military conquest, starvation, drought and over-population. They have been ruled by others depending for their survival on fitting into niches in societies from which they were otherwise racially excluded and on their abilities to evade persecution. These adaptive characteristics may have been created by fierce selection pressures in their life of wandering.

A parallel can be drawn between the Spanish persecutions and that of the Nazis during the years 1933 to 1945. When Hitler came to power he sacked academic teachers with Jewish blood. On May 19th, 1933 the *Manchester Guardian* published a list of 196 professors who had

★ *The Evolution of Man and Society.*

been dismissed their posts in German universities. Nearly 600 Jewish scholars were found jobs in Britain. In 1958 there were 32 'refugees' who were Fellows of the Royal Society, and 17 who were Fellows of the British Academy, while the number of Jewish professors in British Universities was 64. Nuclear physics (and therefore the development of the atom bomb) owed much to Jewish scientists here, and later in Canada and America.

The loss of the six million Jews whom the Nazis exterminated is incalculable—but for the purposes of our discussion it offers another parallel with sixteenth-century Spain. The extermination and exodus of brains and talent from Nazi Germany was indeed great. But those whom Germany lost through emigration were our gain. In totally different circumstances they might even have helped Germany win the war. Certainly Britain, America and the other countries to whom the Jews fled have benefited immensely from their talent.

## THE HUGUENOTS

France was impoverished by the loss of the Huguenots. Like the Jews of Spain the Protestant Huguenots were punished because of their religion. The blow came in 1685 when Louis XIV revoked the Edict of Nantes. Either they recanted or they became a proscribed people. All Protestant ministers were to be expelled from France and had to leave the country within fifteen days. At once the congregations began to emigrate as well as the ministers. Louis, alarmed by the gravity of such a vast loss of talent and skill (the Huguenots were mostly manufacturers: craftsmen and their employers) tried to stem the brain drain but he was too late. Within a few years nearly 350,000 left France. Most went to England, Brandenburg and Holland. About 80,000 came to England and half of these settled eventually in Ireland and the American colonies. Of the half who remained in England, a few at the top of the social strata were outstanding soldiers who officered the four Huguenot regiments serving with William III in the Irish campaign. At the bottom were the modest weavers of Spitalfields who remained inbred for over two centuries preserving their physique and looks (jet black hair, dark eyes), manners and dress, and social characteristics like their friendly societies and flower shows, the pigeon cotes in their roofs and the canaries singing in their rooms. Between these extremes were a varied throng, the offspring of intermarriage with the English—

often with dissenters, sometimes with Anglicans—producing, as Darlington* reminds us, such unexpected hybrid descendants as Sydney Smith, Sir Samuel Romilly, the Attorney-General Edward Bouverie, Pusey, and Cardinal Newman. Thoroughbred Huguenots did not care much about literature and the arts but inter-marriage with the English, 'Yielded in the third generation, England's greatest actor David Garrick, in the fourth our most respected archaeologist Henry Austin Layard and in the sixth . . . Winston Churchill.'

Few Huguenot names in pure-bred state have become household words except perhaps Courtaulds. The biological point here is this. Inbred at home in France the Huguenots were not a very remarkable section of society. Inbred abroad, in England they certainly contributed to the industrial supremacy of England. They introduced the art of calico-printing and wax-bleaching, the weaving of silk, and table linen, and new modes of dyeing. They practically created the glass-making industry and provided the engineering skill to drain the Fens and make harbours. But *outbred*, they yielded over six generations, outstanding new individuals in every field of activity and culture.

It is a historical irony that the Huguenots who fled to Brandenberg were received with open arms for these refugees had a great impact on the iron and steel industry, diverting the Swedish copper which used to go to France to their own workshops. Prussian power was thus fed by the Huguenots who helped to build up a nation destined to become France's deadliest enemy.

The intention of this chapter has been to underline the link between genetics and history. The nation which takes most serious thought for its own genetical future by recognizing and nourishing talent irrespective of colour, politics or religion and understanding that only our parents can provide us with that talent, is most likely to have a future.

* *The Evolution of Man and Society.*

# 28: Mapping Migrations by Blood— 1. The Snags

C AN genetics help us to discover who the English, Irish and Scots are, where they came from and when? Up to a point, especially if genetical data are supported by historical and archaeological evidence. The genetical data that help to map the wanderings of people are the blood group systems, colour blindness and the capacity to taste the chemical phenylthiourea, which to those who can taste it is apparently as bitter as quinine.

The ABO blood group system has been used extensively to make blood group maps of populations all over the world. Each blood type A, B, or O is determined by a single gene which always come in pairs, one from each parent. Thus the blood types in a group of six people could be: AA, AO, OO, OB, BB, AB, depending on the genetic make-up of the parents. The O gene is not as forceful as the others which dominate it, hence AO would give an A reaction, A and B are of equal strength and give an AB reaction; only OO give an O reaction. Each blood type remains fixed for life and each of the genes of the pair is handed on unchanged down the generations.

When blood group data are used for comparative purposes, for

TABLE 17

Frequencies of blood groups O, A, B, and AB in typical populations; Blood-group frequencies are given as percentages.

| Population | Place | Number tested | Blood-group frequency | | | |
|---|---|---|---|---|---|---|
| | | | O | A | B | AB |
| American Indians: | | *Low A, virtually no B* | | | | |
| Toba | Argentina | 194 | 98·5 | 1·5 | 0·0 | 0·0 |
| Sioux | S. Dakota | 100 | 91·0 | 7·0 | 2·0 | 0·0 |
| | | *Moderate A, virtually no B* | | | | |
| Navaho | New Mexico | 359 | 77·7 | 22·5 | 0·0 | 0·0 |
| Pueblo | New Mexico, Jemez, etc. | 310 | 78·4 | 20·0 | 1·6 | 0·0 |
| | | *High A, little B* | | | | |
| Bloods | Montana | 69 | 17·4 | 81·2 | 0·0 | 1·4 |
| Eskimo | Baffin Land | 146 | 55·5 | 43·8 | 0·0 | 0·7 |
| Australian aborigines | S. Australia | 54 | 42·6 | 57·4 | 0·0 | 0·0 |
| Basques | San Sebastian | 91 | 57·2 | 41·7 | 1·1 | 0·0 |
| American Indians: | | | | | | |
| Shoshone | Wyoming | 60 | 51·6 | 45·0 | 1·6 | 1·6 |
| Polynesians | Hawaii | 413 | 36·5 | 60·8 | 2·2 | 0·5 |
| | | *Fairly high A, some B* | | | | |
| West Georgians | Tiflis | 707 | 59·1 | 34·4 | 6·1 | 0·4 |
| English | London | 422 | 47·9 | 42·4 | 8·3 | 1·4 |
| Icelanders | Iceland | 800 | 55·7 | 32·1 | 9·6 | 2·6 |
| French | Paris | 1,265 | 39·8 | 42·3 | 11·8 | 6·1 |
| Armenians | From Turkey | 330 | 27·3 | 53·9 | 12·7 | 6·1 |
| Lapps | Finland | 94 | 33·0 | 52·1 | 12·8 | 2·1 |
| Melanesians | New Guinea | 500 | 37·6 | 44·4 | 13·2 | 4·8 |
| German | Berlin | 39,174 | 36·5 | 42·5 | 14·5 | 6·5 |
| | | *High A and high B* | | | | |
| East Georgians | Tiflis | 1,274 | 36·8 | 42·3 | 15·0 | 5·9 |
| Welsh | North Towns | 192 | 47·9 | 32·8 | 16·2 | 3·1 |
| Italians | Sicily | 540 | 45·9 | 33·4 | 17·3 | 3·4 |
| Siamese | Bangkok | 213 | 37·1 | 17·8 | 35·2 | 9·9 |
| Finns | Häme | 972 | 34·0 | 42·4 | 17·1 | 6·5 |
| Germans | Danzig | 1,888 | 33·1 | 41·6 | 18·0 | 7·3 |
| Ukrainians | Kharkov | 310 | 36·4 | 38·4 | 21·6 | 3·6 |
| Japanese | Tokyo | 29,799 | 30·1 | 38·4 | 21·9 | 9·7 |
| Russians | Near Moscow | 489 | 31·9 | 34·4 | 24·9 | 8·8 |
| Egyptians | Cairo | 502 | 27·3 | 38·5 | 25·5 | 8·8 |
| Egyptians | Assiut | 419 | 24·6 | 34·4 | 31·0 | 10·0 |
| Chinese | Peking | 1,000 | 30·7 | 25·1 | 34·2 | 10·0 |
| Buriats | Near Irkutsk | 1,320 | 32·4 | 20·2 | 39·2 | 8·2 |
| Asiatic Indians | Bengal | 160 | 32·5 | 20·0 | 39·4 | 8·1 |

From 'Genetics and the Human Race' in *Science*, *140*, W. C. Boyd. 1963.

instance to compare a parent with a possible migrant population, it is the *population* which is compared, not individuals. The genetic character of such a population can be measured as a frequency of a sample which is always a mixture of the representatives genes in the group. The blood groups of the English (taken in London in this instance) for example are: 42·4% A, 47·9% O; 8·3% B and 1·4% for the AB group, and this result would be gained by a random sample of say the blood of 1,000 English men and women (see Table 17).

If two separate populations have a similar frequency of ABO groups (and therefore genes) and there is historical evidence for migration, then it is reasonable to conclude that the populations are related genetically and migration has taken place in the past. However, even with similar frequencies care needs to be taken over fanciful speculations about relationships and migrations without historical evidence. It is unnecessary here to summarize all the reasons for this caution but one good one is this: the blood genes we have been describing are subject to natural selection and have been shown to be differently linked with longevity, fertility and disease. People who are 'O' blood group (and thus carry the genes for it) are more susceptible to toxaemia in pregnancy than those who carry an A group; and A's are more prone to broncho-pneumonia than O group or B group people. People who have an AB group have a slight tendency to live longer than those with other groups, while the people with B group might be able to resist bubonic plague and smallpox better than those with other groups. The point is that similarity between blood-group frequencies in two separate populations may be the result not of common ancestry but of convergence caused by similar environments—environments that pick and choose certain people to survive according to their ability to resist certain diseases. This is why blood group data plus archaeological and historical evidence, gives more credibility to a hunch about the origin of a people than either alone. We shall never know the frequency of the common genes in ancient populations whereas archaeological evidence offers at least firm proof of our forebears existence.

# 29: Mapping Migrations by Blood— 2. The Jews

LET us for a moment return to the Jews. They were descended from the people of Ancient Palestine who dispersed in three major waves: the Assyrian Exile in 721 to 530 B.C. when Jews were deported to the Assyrian Empire; the Persian and Greek dispersion in 530 to 70 B.C. when Jews went to the Crimea, Spain, Italy, North Africa and Yemen (there was a Jewish quarter in Alexandria in 330 B.C.); and finally, the Roman Exile following the sacking of Jerusalem in A.D. 70 by Titus and the destruction of the Temple by Hadrian in A.D. 135, when the Jews were dispersed throughout the Roman Empire.

The scattering of the Jews far and wide has apparently had an effect on their 'purity'. A glance at the three blood group charts constructed by Mourant for Jews and non-Jews of North Africa, Europe and Asia show that the Jews are very different genetically (see Fig. 32). If they were all alike in ABO blood groups the circle representing Jewish blood groups would be the same for every country and from this circle lines would radiate in all directions to the points representing non-Jewish populations. If, on the other hand, the Jews were genetically

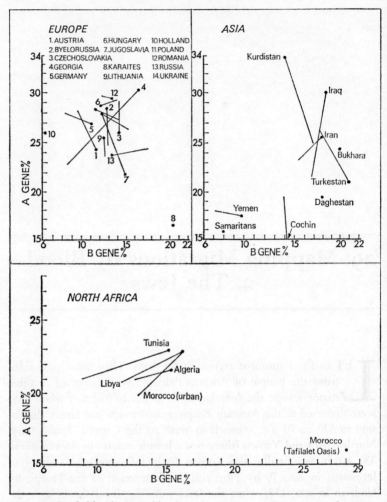

F IG. 32 Jewish blood: ABO blood groups in Jews and non-Jews of Europe, Asia and N. Africa. From an article by A. E. Mourant in *The Genetics of Migrant and Isolate Populations* (ed. E. Goldschmidt), 1963.

identical with the people among whom they live, as the Dutch Jews seem to be, the same circle for a given country would represent Jew and non-Jew and no lines would appear on the diagram. None of the diagrams represents anything like these conditions nor 'half and half' mixtures.

In general it can be said first, that the Jews have kept themselves genetically fairly pure by not inter-marrying too much with nearby non-Jewish people. This generally happens to a migrant people because a country does not ordinarily welcome masses of strangers, especially if they have come with their women and children to stay. The social barriers clang down to isolate the newcomers as much as possible and keep them genetically separate (see Chapter 12). In Europe, however, there is a slight tendency for the ABO frequencies of the Jews in any one country to stray from the average Jewish frequencies in the direction of the frequencies shown by non-Jews in that country. This is probably the result of intermarriage, but it could, *in theory*, be due to the action of natural selection on Jews and non-Jews in a common environment. There is a remarkable uniformity in the blood groups of the Central and European Jews (the Ashkenazim) as a whole and the exiled Spanish Jews (the Sephardim) as a whole. Often these two groups settled side by side as in Holland but they were as different as chalk and cheese. The former, well-to-do, literate, rather haughty, the latter downtrodden. Only in 1812 did legal intermarriage take place, six generations down to the present day compared with the previous fifty generations of separation and separate evolutionary pressures working on them. Indeed in Britain, not until a distinguished Sephardic Jew, Sir Moses Montefiore, friend of Queen Victoria, married a Cohen (an Ashkenazi Jew) was intermarriage accepted. Hence the different gene-frequencies of both groups.

That the Sephardim had kept themselves pure is shown by their high B gene frequency, probably derived from their east Mediterranean ancestors, and not from the Spaniards who have a low B gene frequency. The Ashkenazim have migrated widely and have, as we have noted, hybridized with non-Jews to some extent, but nevertheless maintained their genetic identity more obviously than the mixed hybrid Jews of Asia. In this region non-Jewish communities differ widely in blood groups, and the Jews who have inbred extensively with them reflect these differences.

The Jews then, who have been dispersed from their native land for 1,800 years or more have not been absorbed with the general populations of non-Jews, by intermarriage with them. Why do they differ so much from each other if they came from one country originally and have not interbred with non-Jews to any great extent? Could it be simply, as suggested before that the different selective forces operating in different regions have led to different genetic make-ups in the different populations of Jews? Or might it be, as Darlington suggests, that the Sephardim and the Ashkenazim belonged to different classes in Ancient Palestine; in other words, that each belonged to different 'founder groups' each with different gene frequencies and each fitted into different class positions within the developing class structure of different societies? Both ideas may be correct.

# 30. Mapping Migrations by Blood—
## 3. The British

UNLIKE the Jews, the British are a genetic mix-up with here
and there a pile-up of blood genes which may represent traces
of ancient immigrant populations. It is not surprising that the
British are so mongrel; wave after wave of people drifted, migrated,
fled to, or attacked these shores and outbreeding has shuffled the old
gene combinations. The Old Stone Age people, the first human inhabitants of Britain, got here about 40,000 years ago across the land bridge
which then joined the area to Europe. Then came Matthew Arnold's
'dark Iberians', the black-haired *pre*-Celts from the Mediterranean
about 3700 B.C. It was they who built Stonehenge and Maiden Castle
near Dorchester, buried their dead in communal stone-barrows and
grew their wheat and barley on the high, unwooded chalk downs.
Bronze age people followed them in about 1300 B.C. It was they who
traded Irish gold and copper as far distant as central Europe, worked
Cornish copper and tin and worshipped the sun. The red Celts of fair,
or fiery-red hair and blue eyes (well described by the Romans) arrived
in Britain in about 500 B.C. migrating from overcrowded lands in
North-West Germany and the lands round the Upper Danube. They

NHM—M

were Britain's first iron-smiths and introduced iron ploughshares, horse armour—and the safety pin! A branch of the Celts, the Picts, arrived in eastern Scotland and the Orkneys about 200 B.C. probably from somewhere near the present day Bordeaux and Biarritz. In A.D. 43 came the Roman Invasion under Claudius which lasted until 411. Before this period German migrants from the coast plain north of the Rhine began arriving. These were the Saxons. The Vikings from Denmark, Norway and Sweden, striking from the sea started to plunder and burn Saxon villages and monasteries on the coasts of Northumbria, Scotland, Ireland and Wales from about 800 A.D. onwards. These water-thieves realizing that there was no sea power to defend Britain started to settle permanently and colonized Yorkshire, the East Midlands, and Norfolk. In 1066 came the Normans, themselves descendants of Vikings whose ancestors colonized the mouth of the Seine. In between their coming and that of the very new '1950-onwards' immigrants (see Fig. 34) came others. Religious and political refugees like the Huguenots and Jews and the Dutch and Flemish protestants fleeing from Spanish persecution during Elizabeth's reign, arrived in East Anglia and other centres of the wool trade. In addition to the Jews who escaped from the Inquisition and from Nazi Germany there were the 100,000 Jews who arrived between 1880 and 1905 to escape Russian pogroms and persecution in Eastern Europe. And, of course, people have not only come in, they have emigrated. It has been reckoned that before 1650 100,000 people left Britain for the New World. And as we have seen over 20 million people emigrated from the British Isles, between 1815–1914, 13 million to the States alone.

What can the blood gene map tell us about this ebb and flow of blood? Nothing much about the 'middle period' from the time of William the Conqueror up to the present except that the high proportions of the O blood-group gene in some industrial regions such as South-West Scotland may have been caused by Irish immigration in the nineteenth century. But we are ahead of the story here. Fig. 33 shows the distribution of the ABO blood group in the British Isles and a certain pattern is revealed. There is a high frequency of blood-group gene O in the north-west of the British Isles—in North Wales, in parts of South Wales, in Scotland and the Border Country of England and in Ireland. All these parts have also a patchy distribution of highish B and AB blood-group types. How can this be interpreted? The first clue is one of language. In most of these places Celtic is spoken. The persistence of those languages indicates that these far western and often

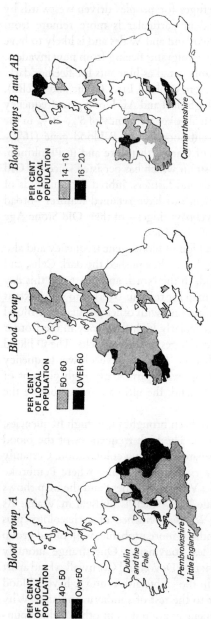

FIG. 33 Mapping migration and survival of ancient races in Britain by blood.

*Blood Group A.* A high proportion of this group probably indicates Anglo-Saxon or Viking settlements, as in Pembrokeshire, which was invaded by Vikings, and in Dublin and the Pale, which were settled in turn by the Normans, then the Flemings, then the English.

*Blood Group O.* A high frequency of O group may indicate Celtic or even older populations. The English are relatively low in this blood group. The high proportion of O in some industrial regions such as southwest Scotland may be because of Irish immigrants. Red hair and O blood group are often associated.

*Blood Groups B and AB* are spread thinly everywhere in Britain. They are slightly more frequent in Scotland, Wales and Ireland—areas associated with the survival of the Celts. Slightly higher concentrations in Carmarthenshire may even be evidence of pre-Celtic people. From *The Observer* Colour Supplement, 19 Feb., 1967.

mountainous areas have been refuges for peoples driven westwards by invaders from the east. Ireland in particular is more remote from Europe than the Highlands of Scotland and Wales and is likely to have been a home for waves of refugee migrants fleeing from new invaders. All these countries, then, probably acted as hideouts for fleeing 'dark' and 'red' Celts (who between them evolved Erse, Gaelic and Welsh). The *dark* Celts probably had a highish B and AB blood gene frequency (14% to 16% compared with an all-over frequency of 5%–10% in the British Isles). The higher concentration of the B blood gene (16%–20%) in the Black Mountains of Carmarthenshire and in Plynlimon, Cardiganshire may represent a strain which has persisted since the Old Stone Age. These hill shepherds and farmers, inbred for hundreds of generations, are believed by Fleure to have retained features—broad faces, strong cheekbones and eyebrow ridges—of their Old Stone Age ancestors, the first inhabitants of these Isles.

The red Celts probably had a high O blood-gene frequency and also genes controlling red or reddish hair. They pushed the dark Celts, and indeed tribes of their own blood, to the North and West. To this day the O blood gene map and the map for red hair overlap to some extent even after eighty generations of mixing with other populations. Blood gene O and red hair show a particularly high frequency in the Border country, Wales and Ireland, old refuges of the red Celts. The O blood gene map in Fig. 33 indicates that the 'English' have a lower frequency of this gene than the Celtic fringe with particularly high pile-ups of the gene in the south-west of Ireland, the ultimate refuge before the Atlantic rollers.

The A blood gene might have been brought in, in high frequencies, by the Vikings or Anglo Saxons. The high frequencies of the blood type in the East may be the remnants of Viking colonization. Certainly archaeological evidence on the peninsula in Wales where Pembroke stands suggests the presence of a Viking settlement and the map shows a high frequency of the A gene here which is unusual in Wales. As suggested earlier, in Chapter 28, the evidence of archaeology plus blood group data makes a hypothesis more probable; with blood group data alone it would be much less convincing. One strange anomaly needs to be mentioned. Why is it that Devon and Cornwall, a land apart where Celtic was still spoken in the eighteenth century, have a blood group pattern which is similar to the rest of southern England? Why is it that the blood group frequencies are not as in other Celtic countries? One suggestion is that Anglo-Saxons settlements from A.D. 450 to

850 smoothed out any genetic discontinuities. Even so fifty or sixty generations is not a long time to create such evenness in the ABO blood genes and detailed studies may well reveal traces of ancient populations.

Let us jump now to the immigrants of the 1950s. In the 1961 census and subsequent estimates there were around 300,000 West Indians, 232,000 Indians and 91,000 Pakistanis in the British Isles. And there are many other minorites (see Fig. 34). How quickly will their genes

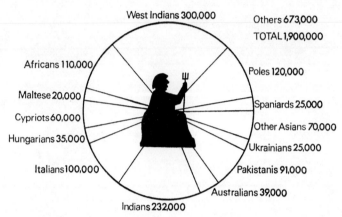

West Indians 300,000
Others 673,000
TOTAL 1,900,000
Africans 110,000
Poles 120,000
Maltese 20,000
Spaniards 25,000
Cypriots 60,000
Other Asians 70,000
Hungarians 35,000
Ukrainians 25,000
Italians 100,000
Pakistanis 91,000
Australians 39,000
Indians 232,000

FIG. 34 Britain's Minorities. There are roughly 1,900,000 foreigners and Commonwealth immigrants living in Britain, apart from one million Irish residents and a floating population of students, au pair girls and tourists. The 'others' include Americans, Canadians, New Zealanders, Germans, French, Scandinavians and Czechs. The approximate figures are based on the 1961 census and estimates of subsequent immigration calculated by the Home Office and by the individual embassies. From *The Observer* Colour Supplement, 19 Feb., 1967.

mix with the already lumpy mixture? If history is any guide, not at all quickly. Race, colour, creed and language are effective barriers to breeding as Chapter 12 showed. In fifty generations a fourth map will be added to the trio above to indicate the state of the mixture— Pakistanis, West Indian, Huguenots, Flemings, Jews, Normans, Anglo Saxons, Vikings, Celts, *pre*-Celts and Stone Age people—who make the British. This map will probably show new patterns as genes settle in new groupings, but pattern there will be and not a smooth mixture.

# Part 6: The Natural History of War

# 31: Extinction and Extermination

**M**OST of this book has been concerned with man's past as an introduction to his present and future. The question to ask now is 'Has man got a future?' Fighting and mass killing of men by men have always been a part of man's natural history (see Tables 18 and 19) but an unprecedented crisis has been reached. Never before in human history has man been capable of destroying himself totally. And yet never before has the possibility of all-out war been so remote. How has this knife-edged situation been reached? If we had to resort to all-out war and drop hydrogen bombs or spread germs, the radiation from bombs dropped on an enemy would affect the attacker and germs might infect the country that delivered them. There would be nowhere to hide.

The mere fact that man is conscious of these problems is revealing of his nature. Most men and most peoples are depressingly aggressive as the candid drawing of a child shows in Fig. 35, and the most urgent problem of human natural history is that of aggression because it is the most lethal of our characteristics and if fully unleashed, could blot out most of the human species in a few days.

What is aggression? Tinbergen defines it as a form of behaviour

TABLE 18
*The Toll of World War 2 (1939–45)* *

| Belligerents (selected countries) | Population (000,000) Based on 1942 figures | Soldiers killed or died (000) | Civilians killed (000) | Total losses in war (000) | Per cent of population killed or died in war |
|---|---|---|---|---|---|
| Germany | 71 | 3,250 | 500 | 3,750 | 5·0 |
| Japan | 72 | 1,507 | 672 | 2,179 | 3·0 |
| U.K. | 48 | 557 | 61 | 618 | 1·3 |
| U.S.S.R. | 175 | 7,500 | 7,500 | 15,000 | 8·6 |
| U.S.A. | 135 | 292 | — | 292 | 0·2 |

* *Total* losses were at least 60,000,000 of which 17,000,000 were military, 34,000,000 were civilian resulting directly from the war and the remainder civilian resulting from war-borne epidemics. Losses distributed over five continents during five years. It has been estimated that in a future war using the bomb, greater losses mainly in Europe and North America would occur in a few days.

From *A Study of War*, Quincy Wright, Chicago, 1965.

TABLE 19
*Proportion of Population of France and Great Britain who Died in War, by Centuries, 1600–1930*

| Century | Deaths in Military Service | Average Annual Deaths in Military Service | Average Population | Death rate | Average Annual Deaths | No. Military Deaths per 1,000 Deaths |
|---|---|---|---|---|---|---|
| | | | France | | | |
| 17th | 673,000 | 6,730 | 18,500,000 | 0·034 | 629,000 | 11 |
| 18th | 1,783,000 | 17,830 | 22,000,000 | 0·030 | 660,000 | 27 |
| 19th | 2,522,000 | 25,220 | 34,000,000 | 0·025 | 850,000 | 30 |
| 20th | 1,427,000 | 42,810 | 40,000,000 | 0·017 | 680,000 | 63 |
| | | | Great Britain | | | |
| 17th | 226,000 | 2,260 | 5,000,000 | 0·030 | 150,000 | 15 |
| 18th | 314,000 | 3,140 | 8,000,000 | 0·028 | 224,000 | 14 |
| 19th | 273,000 | 2,730 | 22,000,000 | 0·022 | 484,000 | 6 |
| 20th | 807,000 | 24,210 | 42,000,000 | 0·012 | 504,000 | 48 |

From *A Study of War*, Quincy Wright, Chicago, 1965.

I Think war should be abolisht
because The VEITNAMESE are
starving itsthe AMRecions
fault And I bet they woyuld
not likthat WEll I serbainly
woyldent. I think the Americanes
sould Be Hunge.

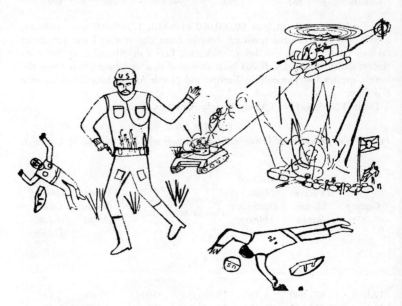

I think that war is a lot
of Rubilish because a lot of people
is geting killed for now reasion
atall I thunk if a war is storted
the two side should find a field
And bight it out and not kill the innocence

FIG. 35 A child's impression of war. From an exhibition reported in *The Times Educational Supplement* 1969.

which tends to remove the opponent, or at least to make him change his behaviour in such a way that he no longer interferes with the attacker. So aggression might mean a shove in the playground, a jab with an elbow at a sale, the use of a flame-thrower or pressing a button to release rockets on a city a thousand miles distant. It could also include the behaviour of men in both sides of a strike maintaining uncompromising attitudes and using heated language. How much of human behaviour in general is learned and how much originates from 'instinctive' or genetically built-in behaviour patterns was discussed in Chapter 4. As far as aggression is concerned, however, the balance of evidence at present favours the Darwinian view that aggression in the past had survival value and hence was selected in genetical evolution. The argument for this view is briefly as follows.

The small groups in which our remote ancestors lived depended on young males to hunt, to fight and to maintain the social order with violence. In war to the death those groups with the most powerful fighters would, to put it in simple terms, leave more offspring than those with timid fighters. In other words aggression had survival value. If the tendency to behave aggressively is heritable, natural selection would favour its spread. And we in the twentieth century may have inherited the biology of aggression that was adaptive in the past.

While most human societies, like the British for example, are reasonably aggressive there do exist others which are notably peaceful. Among these are the Lepchas of Sikkim in the Himalayas and the pygmies of the Ituri rain-forest in the Congo, Polynesian and Melanesian remnants, the gentle Kamaiuras of Brazil and a few others scattered about the world. Geoffrey Gorer writing of these peoples, pinpoints their most significant traits: enormous gusto for concrete physical pleasures—eating, drinking, sex, laughter and little distinction between the ideal characters of men and women. He notes in particular, 'That they have no idea of brave, aggressive masculinity.' But whether these traits are due to learning or instinct is an open question. Those who back the hypothesis that aggression is taught could use these examples to substantiate their claims. Yet selection pressure could have produced all these qualities, particularly in peoples isolated for long periods from war and fighting, thus losing those aggressive behaviours which no longer had survival value. Indeed the peoples mentioned above, the Lepchas, the Ituri pygmies and the Kamaiurs live in inaccessible forests and mountains. In the case of Western man, however, the heroic and the Puritan tradition of the stiff-upper-lip has overridden the effects of selection to what cost we do not yet know. And the same goes for the over-competitive, over-stratified social world in which he lives.

## THE ODD MAN OUT

The study of animal aggression throws into relief one fact about man which makes him different from all other animals. It is that he alone engages in uninhibited mass killing. Other animals when parcelling out their living space into territories or defending their homes against intruders of the same species, rarely engage in fights to the death. Like avoids like. Bloodshed is uncommon. Instead, when they do meet over some territorial dispute they engage in symbolic conflict which is characteristic of each species. Indeed, aeons of time before the Pentagon strategists developed the complicated concepts of 'graduated deterrence', 'controlled war' and 'balances of power' the fish of the warm coral reefs off Florida practised these behaviours bloodlessly and efficiently. When a duelling creature is beaten, it runs, flies, or swims off, chased by the winner. The courage of the fugitive grows stronger as it nears the centre of its territory and it in turn faces to attack the former pursuer. The two eventually come to a point of balance, threatening without fighting. Running away has survival value for, as we know, 'He who fights and runs away, lives to fight another day.' Species who have no fear and fight to the death have in the animal kingdom become extinct. Let man take warning, and let him not be brainwashed or bullied by the heroic tradition into mass suicide.

Territorial behaviour needs a little further elaboration if only to emphasize its complexity, the fact that it varies from species to species, and that it poses many unsolved questions. Curiously, man's *nearest relatives* among the Primates, the savannah monkeys and the great apes appear to be devoid of simple territorial behaviour. As far as man is concerned as it is yet only a hypothesis that he still carries with him the animal heritage of group territoriality—that is the drive to defend property aggressively. If the hypothesis is correct it may have reappeared in early man perhaps with the development of carnivorous habits, the use of weapons, and competition for limited sources of protein.

There is a further point to consider about aggression in man. Lorenz and others have observed that when well-armed animals like wolves, lions and sharp-horned ungulates compete for status or territory, they rarely fight to the death; they have evolved a protective inhibition which prevents them using their ability to kill against their own species. *Poorly armed* creatures like doves or rabbits, on the other hand, have no such inhibition; it is not needed because they are not natural killers. Man seems to have greater affinity with doves and rabbits than with the heavily-armed creatures. We have no stabbing teeth or horns or heavy armour; we are slow moving and thin-skinned. Selection pressure perhaps was not so intensely directed to develop rituals that would prevent us harming each other since we could not easily do so with a fist or a bite. But here is the paradox. Physically weak though we are, our *brains* have made us dangerous. Through our cultural evolution we have become masters of our environment and this has a bearing on aggression in three ways.

## POPULATION PRESSURE, COWARDICE, WEAPONS

In the first place, as we have seen in Part 4 of this book, socio-medical progress has found a way to prolong life and lower the death-rate while allowing reproduction to continue in excess of the death-rate. But neither our resources nor the sheer space for living increases in proportion to our expanding population. The result is that we now live at a much higher density than that in which genetic evolution moulded us (see Chapter 14). This factor, together with the expansion of our environments with every new scientific discovery leads to greater overlap between the 'territories' of different nations and power blocks with ever fiercer competition. Such ever-increasing overlap leads to continuous inter-group contacts and to continuous external provocation. Human populations are thus 'ecologically unstable': that is they are still expanding their ranges. When an animal population invades a new area it increases up to an optimum density and then oscillates in numbers around this value which is related to the carrying capacity of the particular environment. If the population continues to expand it can be described as unstable (and most human populations have been doing just this for the last few hundred years). Such expansion in animals will lead to the sort of fighting already described which establishes a winner and a loser with little loss of life. Most human fighting appears to take place in unstable ecological circumstances but with characteristic loss of life.

There is a further ecological point which needs bringing out here.

Although it is true that we are a single species in that breeding can take place between all the varieties of men, *culturally* men are very varied; they occupy many different ecological niches each with different behaviour patterns associated with them. Ecologically then human populations can act like *different* species. Now among animal species there is often a considerable amount of fighting between close ecological competitors and this has a human parallel: much human warfare has been due to competition between different cultures for the same area.

Secondly, if man carries with him traces of his animal heritage of group territoriality—and this as we have noted is by no means proved —and if a weak army is attacked by a stronger one, the weaker should by all accounts turn and run. But most peoples who have been brought up with strong 'heroic' or religious or political beliefs would not dare to turn tail. They would be shot for cowardice or lose face or become outcasts. Animals would run because the behaviour has survival value but our traditions prevent us. There is a struggle within us; our 'instinct' (controlled by the brain stem) and our 'reason' (controlled by the brain cortex) appears to be at logger-heads.

Last, although we are physically weak, our ability to invent, make, and use tools has made slaughter easy. A club is more effective than a fist and a spear better than a club. Even more deadly is push-button warfare because the 'distress signals' of opponents—their submissive gestures, pitiful expressions and pleading voices—which inhibit animals from killing, and sometimes persuade human beings to hold their hand, cannot be seen.

All three facets of our cultures: the population explosion leading to ecological instability, the heroic tradition and the invention of our war machines have helped us, as Tinbergen suggests, to become 'unhinged killers', on the one hand we seem to have only a weakly built-in control to the unleashing of our aggression, yet our brain and hands have evolved the most powerful killing instruments.

## THE PROPER STUDY OF MANKIND IS RATS?

According to Tinbergen one basic conclusion about aggression is admissable at present: further research in animal behaviour is urgently needed for clarifying problems of human behaviour, particularly that of aggression. A basic question needs to be answered, 'What makes men attack each other?' And other questions stem from this: 'Is the readiness to attack constant or not?', 'What are the stimuli, both external and internal that trigger fighting?' and, 'What happens to the hormone balance and other physiological variables inside us at the brink of a fight or on the eve of war?' Readiness to start a fight is clearly variable. In some instances hunger tends to cause an increase in fighting among animals when there is competition for food. There is also evidence of animals becoming aggressive because of overcrowding. Then much experimental work with birds and mammals has shown that testosterone, the male hormone, when administered, lowers the threshold for aggression. The ranking positions in starlings can be altered by doses of luteinizing hormones; those given the hormone improve their position. On this score then, aggression is not a 'penny-in-the-slot' phenomenon but caused by the interplay of a number of internal and external factors. If we can answer these questions fully and eventually develop a theory of aggression for animals, we might in time be able to alter external and internal conditions to avoid aggression in man, in individuals if not in populations.

Perhaps, however, all this research on animal behaviour described above sheds but a fitful light on human aggression because it can take no account of language which is exclusively human. Man, because of his cortex, the human 'thinking cap', as Koestler calls it, has the 'dangerous privilege' of using words to coin battle cries, invent war slogans, write eve-of-battle speeches, formulate doctrines and belief systems which can be used to whip up group feeling against other groups who may differ in language and beliefs (and colour). Research into animal behaviour cannot be compared in these terms. Commonsense dictates, however, that a reasonably sure way to minimize aggression is to bring down population size and to stop poisoning and fouling our habitat.

## ERASING OF DIVERSITY

This chapter would not be complete without mention of another form of brutal aggression—wars of extermination. This matter is relevant to this book because primitive peoples have been and are being exterminated on a vast scale, often by land-hungry whites who treat them like vermin. Apart from the extraordinary cruelty involved, such extermination leads to irreversible loss. It is as if rare books have been removed from a rich library and burnt. Norman Lewis writing of the extermination of the Indians in Brazil in recent years describes some of the surviving tribes as, 'Giants with herculean limbs, armed with immense long bows of the kind an archer at Crecy might have used. A few groups are ethnically mysterious with blue eyes and fairish hair . . . one common factor unites them all—a brilliant fitness for survival.' (see Chapter 11 and 12).

These Brazilian tribes, widespread in the sixteenth century were decimated by the Conquistadores who hanged them, burnt them in heaps, burned them alive, had them torn to pieces by fierce dogs or flung alive over cliffs. It is thought that about 12 million of these tribesmen were killed. Now, in twentieth-century Brazil and elsewhere in South America, the slaughter goes on—by bullets, machetes, food laced with arsenic and clothes impregnated with the virus of smallpox. Perhaps only 50,000 to 100,000 of these diverse peoples are left, each tribe sometimes of only a few hundreds, with its own language, customs and organization and each with a detailed knowledge of the habitat. And nearly all these tribes are often of the highest intelligence and may possess a genius for invention and action totally different from our own. Only by protecting them in their own territories as we would jealously guard any wild creature, shall we be able to prevent their destruction and with that, the loss of the opportunity of studying their conditions of life, their knowledge of medicines, their art and language. Without them the natural history of man would be the poorer.

# Bibliography

*An asterisk (★) indicates books and papers suitable for the non-specialist*

## PART I. MECHANICS OF NATURAL HISTORY

Carter, C. O., 'Changing patterns of differential fertility in Northwest Europe and in North America', *Eugen Quart*, 9, 1962.

Clarke, C., 'World Population', *Nature* **181**, 1958.

★Hall, Peter, 'The Megabirth Nightmare', *Sunday Times Magazine*, March 20th, 1966.

Meade, J. E. & Parkes, A. S. (ed.), *Biological Aspects of Social Problems*, Oliver & Boyd, 1965.

*United Nations Demographic Year Books*, 1961, 1963.

Registrar General's Statistical Review of England and Wales for 1967. Part II. *Population Tables*, H.M.S.O.

*Man and his Environment*, B.B.C. Publications, 1964.

## PART II. THE AMATEUR OF ANIMALS

★Cannon, W. B., *The Wisdom of the Body*, Norton, New York, 1932.

Darlington, C. D., 'Psychology, genetics & the process of history', *Brit. J. Psychol.*, **54**, 4, 1963.

★—— *Genetics & Man*, Penguin, 1966.

Harrison, G. A. *et al. Human Biology*, O.U.P., 1964.

Stern, C., *Principles of Human Genetics*, Freeman, 1960.


PART III. MAN'S PAST

Baker, P. T. & Weiner, J. S. (ed.), *The Biology of Human Adaptability*, O.U.P. 1966.

*Braidwood, R. J., 'The Agricultural Revolution', *Scientific American*, **203**, 1960.

Burkhill, I. H. 'The Greater yam in the service of man', *Adv. Sci.*, 7, 1951.

*Campbell, B., *Human Evolution*, Heinemann Educational Books, 1967.

*Carr-Saunders, A. M., *The Population Problem*, O.U.P., 1922.

*Childe, V. G., *What Happened in History*, Penguin, 1942.

Clarke, C., 'Demographic Problems on a World Scale', *World Justice* No. 4, 1965.

*Cole, S., 'The Neolithic Revolution', *Brit. Museum*, Natural History, 1967.

Coon, C. S., *The Origin of Races*, Cape, 1963.

*—— *The Living Races of Man*, Cape, 1966.

Darlington, C. D., 'The Control of Evolution in Man', *Eugenics Review*, **50**, 3, 1958.

—— 'The Control of Evolution in Man', *Nature*, **182**, 1958.

—— 'Cousin Marriage and the Evolution of the Breeding System in Man, *Heredity*, **14**, 1960.

—— 'The Future of Man', *Heredity*, **15**, 1960.

—— *Chromosome Botany and the Origins of Cultivated Plants*, Allen & Unwin, 1963.

—— 'Contending with evolution', Essay Review, *Science Progress*, **52**, 1964.

*——(ed Robert E. Kuttner) (published as Human Society & Genetics) in *Race and Modern Science*, Social Science Press, New York, 1967.

*—— *The Evolution of Man & Society*, Allen & Unwin, 1969.

*De Beer Gavin, *Atlas of Evolution*, Nelson, 1964.

Goodhart, C. B., 'World population growth and its regulation by natural means', *Nature*, **178**, 1956.

*Howells, William, *Mankind in the Making*, Secker, 1960.

*Isaac, E., 'On the domestication of cattle', *Science*, **137**, 1962.

*Morris, Desmond, *The Naked Ape*, Cape, 1967.

*Sears, P. B., *The Ecology of Man*, Annual Report Smithsonian Institution, 1958.

*Sahlins, M. D., 'The Origin of Society' *Scientific American*, **203**, No. 3, 1960.

Thomas, W. L. (ed), *Man's Role in Changing the Face of the Earth*, Chicago U.P., 1956.

*Washburn, *et al.*, 'Field Studies of Old World Monkeys and Apes', *Science*, **150**, 1965.

## PART IV. CHANGING DISEASE PATTERNS

★Brockington, F., *World Health*, Churchill, 1967.

Brownlee, J. R., 'The history of the birth and death rates in England and Wales taken as a whole from 1750 to the present time', *Public Health*, Vol. XIX, 1916.

★Burnet, M., *The Natural History of Infectious Diseases*, C.U.P., 1953.

Creighton, C., *A History of Epidemics in Britain*, Vols. 1 & 2, Cambridge, 1894.

Henderson, P., 'Changing Patterns of Disease and Disability in Schoolchildren in England and Wales', *B.M.J.*, **2**, 1968

Howe, M., *National Atlas of Disease Mortality in the U.K.*, Royal Geographical Society, 1958.

Johnson, G., 'Health conditions in rural and urban areas of developing countries', *Population Studies*, XVII, 1964.

★Logan, R. F. L., 'Health Hazards', in *Middle Age*, B.B.C. publications, 1967

Logan, W. P. D., Mortality in England and Wales from 1848 to 1947, *Population Studies*, IV, 1950.

McKeown, T. & Brown, R. G., Medical Evidence related to English population changes in the eighteenth century, *Population Studies*, Vol. IX, 1955.

McKeown, T. & Brown, R. G., 'Reasons for the decline of mortality in England and Wales during the nineteenth century, *Population Studies*, XVI, 1962.

★Medawar, P. B., *The Future of Man*, Methuen, 1960.

★Morris, J. N., *The Uses of Epidemiology*, Livingstone, 1964.

★Platt, the Lord & Parkes, A. S., *Social and Genetic Influences on Life and Death*, Oliver & Boyd, 1967.

Roberts, R. S., 'Epidemics and Social History', Essay Review in *Medical History*, xii, 1968.

★Sauvy, A., *Fertility and Survival*, Chatto & Windus, 1967.

Wolstenholme, G. (ed), *Health of Mankind*, C.I.B.A. Foundation, 1967.

★Ziegler, Philip, *The Black Death*, Collins, 1969.

*On the State of the Public Health*, Reports from 1920 Min. of Health.

★Coronary disease and competitiveness. Leading article in *B.M.J.*, **1**, 1969.


## PART V. THE BRAIN AND BRAWN DRAIN

Darlington, C. D., 'Control of evolution in man', *Nature*, **182**, 1958.

★——, *The Evolution of Man & Society*, Allen & Unwin, 1969.

★De Beer, G., *Genetics and Pre-History*, Rede Lecture, C.U.P., 1965.

★Galton, F., *Hereditary Genius*, Fontana, 1869.

Goldschmidt, E. (ed), *The Genetics of Migrant and Isolate Populations*, Williams & Wilkins, 1963.

Hansen, M. L., *The Atlantic Migration*, Harvard, 1951.

Lee, J. A. H., 'Regional variations in intellectual ability in Britain', *Eugenics Review*, April, 1957.

*Lynn, R., 'Genetics of the Brain Drain', *Economic Age* (January), 1969.

Mourant, A. E., *The Distribution of the Human Blood Groups*, Blackwell, 1954.

Scott, P., 'An isonoetic map of Tasmania', *Geog. Review*, July, 1957.

Stern, C., *Principals of Human Genetics*, Freeman, 1960.

*Trevelyan, G. M., *A Shortened History of England*, Pelican, 1959.

*'Who are the English', *Observer* Colour Supplement, Feb., 1967.

## PART VI. WAR AND EXTINCTION

Berkowitz, L., *Aggression: a Social Psychological Analysis*, McGraw Hill, 1962.

Blackett, P. M. S., *Advancement of Science*, **15**, 1959.

*Koestler, A., 'The Urge to Self-destruction', *The Observer*, 28 Sept., 1969.

*Lorenz, K., *On Aggression*, Methuen, 1966.

*Lewis, Norman, 'Genocide', *Sunday Times* Colour Supplement, Feb. 23rd, 1969.

*Montague, M. F. Ashley, *Man and Aggression*, Oxford, 1969.

Morton Fried, *et al.* (eds), *The Anthropology of Armed Conflict and Aggression*, Nat. Hist. Press, N. York (especially the chapter by Frank Livingstone), 1968.

Pringle, J. W. S., 'The Treasure House of Nature', *Advancement of Science*, Vol. 23, No. 112, 1966.

*Russell, C. & W. M. S., *Violence, Monkeys and Men*, Macmillan, 1968.

Southwick, C. H., 'An experimental study of intragroup agonistic behaviour in rhesus monkeys', *Behaviour*, **28**, 1967.

*Storr, A., *Human Aggression*, Allen Lane, 1968.

*Tinbergen, N., 'On War and Peace in Animals and Men', *Science*, 1968.

# Index